OXFORDSHIRE COUN

7

THE IRONSTONE HILLS

GREAT TEW TO BANBURY

MARY WEBB   ALAN SPICER
ALLISTER SMITH

Illustrated by LOUISE SPICER

THE
aRTISAN
PRESS

The Artisan Press (Publishers) Limited

Cover photograph: Ironstone cottages, Wroxton
(Alan Spicer)

PUBLISHER'S NOTE

The routes of the walks in this book all follow definitive rights of way and have been checked by Oxfordshire County Council's Countryside Service. It is advisable for walkers to use the latest edition of the relevant Ordnance Survey Pathfinder Series 1:25000 scale maps to follow the route of the walks. Diversions to the definitive right of way may occur and walkers should look out for signs notifying official diversions. Enquiries regarding rights of way should be addressed to the Countryside Service, Oxfordshire County Council, Holton, Oxford OX33 1QQ

Oxfordshire Country Walks – Vol. 7: The Ironstone Hills
ISBN 0 9529238 5 8
First published in 2000 by The Artisan Press (Publishers) Ltd
Copyright © 2000 The Artisan Press (Publishers) Ltd

A CIP catalogue record for this book is available from the British Library.

Typesetting and origination by The Artisan Press (Publishers) Ltd.
Printed by Information Press, Eynsham, Oxon

The Artisan Press (Publishers) Ltd
PO Box 1568, Wedmore, Somerset BS28 4YE
and The Old Fire Station, Charlbury, Oxon OX7 3QW

Contents

Foreword

The prime focus of the Council for the Protection of Rural England is the English landscape; its beauty, diversity, and tranquillity. Our work is increasingly aimed at finding solutions, rather than just highlighting concerns, and constructively influencing decisions that will maintain a feeling of balance, of harmony (man with nature), and above all of continuity in the landscape. We are all aware of the remorseless pressures on much of our countryside from more houses, more traffic, more noise, and especially since 1945 from malpractice in modern farming and forestry. There is a growing feeling amongst many that as the diversity and richness of the countryside is diminished, so we ourselves are diminished.

Happily in Oxfordshire we are fortunate to have still a living and working countryside (over 75% of the County remains rural), which retains many of our cherished values. Better still, the public is able, largely through earlier work by the CPRE with the Oxfordshire County Council, to enjoy quietly its pleasures at first hand through an excellent network of footpaths and bridleways. We are delighted therefore to continue our support for the Oxfordshire Country Walks series, and we hope that this latest guide, which covers the North of the County, will do much to increase the pleasures of exploring at its best the special character of this unique part of middle England.

BRUCE TREMAYNE
Chairman of CPRE Oxfordshire Branch

If you would like to join CPRE you will find an application form at the back of this book. For further information please contact:

CPRE Oxfordshire Branch,
60 East St Helen Street, Abingdon, Oxfordshire OX14 5EB
Tel/fax: 01235 535900   email: oxoncpre@globalnet.co.uk

CPRE

Your countryside – your voice

Preface

This series of walks is based in the Ironstone Country of North Oxfordshire and explores the landscape between the County boundary to the west and the Cherwell Valley to the east.

This is a fertile agricultural region with attractive villages and peaceful hillsides and valleys. Some of the walks pass through historic parklands, others follow quiet lanes, fieldpaths and ancient ridgeways providing extensive views over this unspoilt countryside.

The length of the walks varies from three to eight miles. There are some short steep climbs on many of the routes given the undulating terrain. Some low-lying areas can be very muddy following heavy rainfall or after ploughing. Comments on the condition of each walk precedes each set of route descriptions.

This guide has been produced with the aim of showing how much of our history, both natural and human, is present in the landscape.

Features such as Iron Age camps, Roman roads, remains of Norman castles and fortified manor houses are reminders of the history of the settlement of this area. Ridge and furrow patterns, ancient trackways, water mills, turnpike roads, disused railways and quarries are evidence of past farming methods, transport routes and industries.

All these signposts to the past can be seen today within the context of a modern agricultural landscape, which still contains remnant areas of more natural habitats.

Introduction

This book covers an approximately diamond-shaped area between Wroxton in the north, Hook Norton in the west, Deddington in the east, and Great Tew to the south. Although close to Banbury and the M40, this is a peaceful area with small villages and an agricultural landscape of hills and valleys. Although these appear timeless, there have been major changes over time, influenced by both natural and human forces. Traces of earlier landscapes can still be found today, some more apparent than others, but all helping us to understand the countryside we see today.

GEOLOGY

This area has a distinctive geology, which is demonstrated by the colour of the local stone and soil and which led to the name of the Redlands for the district. Between 140 to 195 million years ago during the Jurassic period, shallow seas covered the land, alternating between sea, swamp, land or lakes. The underlying crust slowly warped and this led to variation in the depth of the water which determined the types of deposits laid down. In deeper water, dark muds were deposited which formed the Lias clay, whilst in shallower water iron-rich and calcareous sediments were deposited.

These layers can be divided into three types, the Lower, Middle and Upper Lias. These rock formations are the oldest visible in the county. The Lower Lias underlies the whole county but only appears as clay at the surface in the far north, outside our area, where it has been used for local brick making, and in the river valleys of the Cherwell and Evenlode.

The Middle Lias is divided into two types. The lower layers consist of sands and silts, while the upper layer is the Marlstone Rock Bed. This contains iron in varying amounts ranging from a rusty calcareous sandstone in which the iron is only sufficient to colour the stone the characteristic dark golden colour of the area, to an iron-ore which contains up to 30% iron in an oolitic limestone. It is this strata which has had the most influence on this part of Oxfordshire.

The Upper Lias is clay with some occurrences of thin bands of limestone which contains many fossils, especially ammonites.

In the south of our area is a thin layer of Lower Oolitic limestone which was deposited on top of the Lias layer. This paler limestone, characteristic of the Cotswolds, extends as far north as Hook Norton and Tadmarton becoming more sandy in these areas, so much so that it is known as Northampton Sands. It is found as the capping of many of the hills, overlying the Upper Lias.

During the Ice Ages, the ice sheets banked up against the ridge of the Cotswolds, but melt water flowed over this area, dissecting valleys in a south-easterly direction. These valleys are much deeper than would be expected from the present flow of water, probably indicating the action of glacial melt water. Deposits carried by this huge volume of water further altered the landscape, sometimes filling valleys as occurred south-west of Shutford near Farmington Farm.

The variation in the underlying geology leads to the shape of the landscape seen today. The thin layer of Lower Oolitic limestone results in the landscape of separate hills and small valleys. Examples include Round Hill, Jester's Hill and Madmarston Camp (Walk 3), very different to the more rolling landscape of the Cotswolds further south and west where the limestone is very much thicker and more resistant to erosion. The ironstone or Marlstone outcrops have had the most obvious effect on the locality. The rich red-brown soil, formed from naturally weathered stone, has been renowned for centuries for its fertility, while the stone itself has been quarried and used in building, again for many centuries. The iron-rich stone was quarried from the mid 19th century up to the late 1960's for production of iron. The sandy deposits have also been used for building materials.

Sometimes there is a sudden transition between different types of soil or rock. There are several small fault lines in this area where the layers of different rock have moved relative to each other – see Walk 8.

The underlying clay beneath the various types of sandstone or limestone forms an impermeable layer. Water, which penetrates the porous limestone, meets this clay barrier and emerges as a spring. There is often a well defined line of springs along a valley slope, showing where the two strata meet. The abundance of water has had an effect on the landscape, both by the action of water in forming valleys and by influencing settlement pattern. Before mains water was available, the situation of human habitation depended on the availability of water. The presence of a spring or permanent stream would have been an important factor in choosing a settlement site. As you walk through this area, notice the pattern of settlements; many are built below the hill tops but above the valley bottom, so ensuring the availability of both water and a variety of soil types.

LANDSCAPE AND AGRICULTURE

The landscape of today is based on the settlement and farming patterns of the past and in many places mentioned in this book, remnants can be found in the modern countryside. As in most parts of England there has been continuous human habitation in this area for at least 5,000 years. The dry limestone ridges, used as communication routes, and the plentiful water supply would have been attractive to prehistoric man, although there are few tangible remains today. The most obvious are the Iron Age camps at Ilbury, Tadmarton Heath and Madmarston, the latter being occupied for almost three centuries from 200 B.C. The Romans had a greater impact and had a settlement at Swalcliffe Lea, close to Madmarston. There were also smaller villages dotted through the area. Several Roman roads can be traced such as the route from Droitwich which led to the Lea settlement. After the Roman period, settlement by the Saxons was early in this area, again probably because of the good soil and plentiful water. Many of the place-names are linked to personal names which suggest this early presence (Walks 4, 5 and 7).

By the time of the Norman Conquest and the making of the Domesday Book in 1086, settlements and agriculture were well established. The Redlands supported the highest population and were the most cultivated part of the county. It was a wealthy area based on the rich corn-growing land where the plentiful water encouraged the use of water mills. There was little woodland but much meadow land, situated along the banks of rivers and streams.

All through the Middles Ages the Redlands area had a mixed agricultural economy rather than being dependant on sheep husbandry, which was prevalent in the Cotswolds in the latter part of this period. Villages had two large open fields, which were farmed in common being divided into strips allotted to each family. Ploughing with cumbersome ox teams built up a system of large ridges and furrows in the soil which helped drainage. These ridges have a distinctive reversed-S shape which can often still be seen. When the population was at its peak, in the early 14th century, steeper land was brought into cultivation. Here ploughing followed the contours of the slope and led to the formation of terraces known as lynchets. However this was quickly abandoned as the population plummeted due to the ravages of the Black Death around 1348. Remains of both these features can be found along these walks, the best examples being around Wigginton (Walk 5) and Ilbury (Walk 7).

A feature of this district was the further division of the land into two separate sets of field systems, called Ends, as happened at Duns Tew and Deddington. In other places, each large open field was divided into "quarters".

This led to greater flexibility in the use of the land so that a greater mix of crops could be grown. A later feature was the intermingling of grass "leys" within the arable, which would often be temporarily enclosed and manured by sheep or other animals. After several years, they would be ploughed again for arable crops, when other land was put down to grass.

There was very little early inclosure for specialised agriculture, most parishes remained set amongst open fields until parliamentary inclosure in the 18th and early 19th centuries. There were often a few small old hedged fields around the villages, or where the lord of the manor enclosed his own land or demesne (Walk 7). The hamlet of Ilbury (Walk 7) was an exception with inclosed fields as early as the 14th century which were used as sheep pasture. At Broughton (Walk 2) all the open fields were inclosed at the end of the 16th century, when arable gave way to sheep and cattle pasture, the first parish to have a major landscape change. Here it was at the behest of the Lord of the Manor but later inclosure had to be agreed by individual Acts of Parliament for each parish. The Lord of the Manor and other large landowners were the instigators of change as they had the most to gain from inclosure and the labourers were often badly affected as they lost their rights to common land. Inclosure had a dramatic effect on the landscape, changing the open spaces to smaller rectangular fields laid out by the surveyor who planned the re-allocation of land. The fields were hedged with hawthorn or blackthorn often with standard oak, elm or ash trees planted at the same time; more rarely other shrubs were used such as crab apple (Walk 8). On higher ground dry stone walls were built. New farms were built, away from the villages, situated in isolation amongst the new fields (Walk 8). In several villages, remnants of the old farms can be seen, as prior to inclosure, farm houses and buildings were within the village.

In this area, despite its wealth, the impact made by large landowners was quite small compared to some other parts of Oxfordshire (see Book 5 Glyme Valley). Landscaped pleasure grounds or parks were on a relatively modest scale, as at Wroxton, Swalcliffe and Broughton. Horace Walpole was quite scathing in his comments about Wroxton's garden when he visited in the mid 18th century admiring only the lake and cascade. The landscape at Broughton must have been a novelty in the area when the fields were inclosed in the late 16th century but the later park was quite small scale. The only estate where the landscape was dramatically altered was that at Great Tew where, in the early 19th century, there was a complete redesign of the estate by John Loudon who worked there for three years. This included not only an ornamental park but also a model farm and farmland, all designed to be attractive as well as productive (Walk 6).

By the early 20th century, mixed farming was still successful in the Redlands area. However, due to the isolation of many villages from the railways, the use of feed or fertilizer from outside the district was not profitable. For the same reason, produce such as milk was not sent away to London as happened further south or east. Instead milk was made into butter, which keeps well, and sent to Birmingham.

This is the landscape we see today, although now there are more gradual changes as hedges are grubbed out to make larger fields which are needed to allow the use of large modern machinery. In some places though hedges are now being replaced, often in conjunction with tree planting in strips or across field corners, so that in time the landscape will change again as these trees mature. The old pattern of grazing in the river valleys and arable crops on the higher land is still noticeable, although probably not as marked as in the past.

LANDSCAPE AND INDUSTRY

As mentioned above, the underlying Marlstone or ironstone has a marked effect on the Redlands area. The stone is easily worked and has been used as a building material for many centuries. There are a good number of excellent examples of vernacular architecture in every village. Much of the stone was quarried in the villages,

and the wealth from farming allowed the building of many yeoman houses between the 16th and the 18th century, replacing the old timber framed dwellings. The colour and quality of the stone varies from place to place, ranging from good quality square blocks or ashlar to narrow small rubble-like stone. Most houses were thatched or roofed with Stonesfield slate (see Book 1, Evenlode and Wychwood) but the development in the late 18th century of the Oxford Canal through Banbury gave access to materials from further afield so that Welsh slates can also be seen in the area, though to a lesser extent.

Ironstone and thatch, Great Tew cottages

The stone was quarried to produce iron from the mid 19th century in Wroxton and Hook Norton (Walks 1 and 5). The Brymbo Iron works were founded in Hook Norton in 1896. The ore was calcined by heating strongly, which removed the water content and reduced it to red iron oxide, when it was sent for smelting elsewhere. The ore was close to the surface, so the impact from this industry was lessened as the workings could be easily back filled. The development of this industry was accelerated by the opening of good transport links to the industrial Midlands by railway. Now there is only one quarry left, situated north of this area.

The proximity to the wool produced in the Cotswolds resulted in a tradition of weaving around the Banbury area. A specialised weaving industry grew up in Banbury and surrounding villages such as Deddington, Broughton, Shutford and Wroxton from about 1750. Plush, a fabric similar to velvet but with a longer pile, was made from a variety of fibres including wool, silk and cotton or mixtures of these. It had many uses ranging from livery to household items such as curtains and upholstery. North Oxfordshire embossed plush was sent all over the world, to royal courts through Europe and as far as Japan where it was used for winter-weight kimonos. Locally it was used at Broughton Castle as upholstery fabric. The industry gradually declined after about 1850 because of competition from power loom weaving in Coventry. The last working factory was in Shutford which finally closed in 1948.

Another industry which developed in this area was not only related to the woollen trade but also was dependant on the water which flowed from the spring line at the base of the porous rock layer (see above). The plentiful running water was used in the fulling process which converts soft woven fabric into a firmer material. This was done by treading the fabric in water; later water-driven wooden hammers were used. Now the process is done mechanically with rollers. There were several fulling mills in this area, notably in Broughton (Walk 2).

LANDSCAPE AND WILDLIFE

The changes over the centuries in the landscape and its management have not only affected its appearance but the wild life which depends on varied habitats throughout the countryside.

The gradual abandonment of the open field system with its associated areas of commonland and heath must have had a marked effect on the abundance and distribution of the more specialised plants, birds and animals which needed specific conditions to thrive.

Rigorous control of so-called "vermin" species of birds and mammals, perceived to be predators of game, together with the interests of egg and insect collectors, and the fashionable use of plumage, also led to great reductions and even extinctions of some birds, insects and ferns in the 19th century.

The ploughing of old meadow and pasture to grow more food during the Second World War severely reduced these habitats. The post-war period of intensification of arable farming followed the development of pesticides, artificial fertilizers and the improved mechanisation of farm work. Together with the replacement of hay making with silage production, the drainage of wetlands and hedgerow removal made the land more easily worked and more productive.

These changes in farming practices had a dramatic effect on both landscape and wildlife. Today only about 8% of Oxfordshire's countryside is considered to be of high nature conservation value and only 2% has some form of statutory protection. In the Ironstone Country, ancient species-rich woodland is virtually non-existent and only small isolated fragments of limestone grassland, heath, marsh and wet grassland remain.

RELIC HABITATS IN FORMER LANDSCAPES

Fortunately, a few remnants of particular habitats survive in this area as links with past landscapes. This allows some typical as well as rare plants and animals to survive, although their future may be in question due to their isolation and increasing environmental pressures. In 1998 the Oxfordshire Nature Conservation Forum, an informal partnership of over 50 local and national organisations co-ordinated the production of "Action for Wildlife", Oxfordshire's Biodiversity Action Plan. This identifies scarce habitats and threatened wildlife species and specifies appropriate mechanisms to conserve and where possible enhance wildlife resources.

In this part of the county, significant areas of **heathland** existed two hundred years ago, particularly around Sibford, Tadmarton, Wigginton and Swerford. Today the vast majority of this habitat no longer exists, in common with the rest of lowland England where 80% of heath has been lost during this period. However in the tiny fragments of heath or acid grassland, as found at Tadmarton, gorse, bracken and small patches of heather survive but are probably too small to support characteristic species such as the tree pipit, nightjar or adder.

Limestone grassland, with its rich assemblage of flowering plants tolerant of a limy soil and drier conditions, is a haven for many insects, including butterflies attracted by the supply of nectar. Although only a few areas are to be seen in this region, several roadside verges, steep banks and narrow bands alongside tracks and footpaths contain fragments of this scarce habitat. Protected from ploughing and spraying, this "unimproved " grassland has also survived in a number of local churchyards, archaeological sites and on the banks of disused railway lines. Typical flora to be seen on these walks include salad burnet, bird's-foot-trefoil, thyme, greater knapweed and lady's bedstraw.

Greater knapweed

Wetlands in this area are represented by the River Swere and the Sor Brook, both tributaries of the River Cherwell, a few lakes and ponds, and some small areas of marsh and wet meadow which have escaped drainage. The Cherwell Valley lies at the eastern edge of the ironstone country with larger areas of marsh and damp grassland adjacent to the watery corridor of the river and the Oxford Canal. This is part of the Upper Thames Tributaries Environmentally Sensitive Area and contains many wetland plants, insects and both breeding and resident birds, including kingfisher, snipe, lapwing, water rail, sedge warbler and little grebe. Conservation programmes involving monitoring and habitat improvement are aimed at recolonising these wetlands with the otter and water vole. If successful,

Snipe

further colonisation might follow into the adjacent wetland areas of the ironstone country by these and other aquatic wildlife.

Only a very few **woodlands** in this landscape are older than about 200 years, Worton Wood being one exception. Most are relatively small areas of conifers or hardwoods planted as coverts for gamebirds or foxes, or to yield commercial timber. Ornamental woodlands and specimen trees decorate the parklands of Great Tew, Wroxton and Broughton. New areas of mixed deciduous trees planted by landowners and conservation bodies are on the increase and will enhance the landscape of the 21st century. Hedgerows, to some extent, substitute for woodland, resembling woodland edge habitat in their provision of food stores, shelter and breeding niches for a range of birds, mammals and insects. Larger trees within the hedgerow attract insectivorous birds and provide holes and crevices for nesting owls, woodpeckers, kestrels, treecreepers and nuthatches. Hedges on grassy banks or close to streams offer extra shelter and food supplies to grass snakes, bank voles, shrews and other mammals and insects. Continuous networks of thick hedgerows provide cover for these creatures, enabling them to search for food without being detected by their predators.

Human habitats, such as gardens, churchyards, cottages and farm buildings may support a wide range of wildlife. To some extent they can substitute for the loss of natural habitats such as wildflower meadows, trees and hedgerows in the surrounding countryside. Buildings with wide eaves will attract nest-building house martins while swallows and barn owls will occupy stables and barns. Bats will roost in church towers, house roofs and disused railway tunnels. The stonework of drystone walls, cottages, churches and graveyards are often covered by a variety of colourful lichens, mosses, ferns and small plants such as ivy-leaved toadflax. Gardens can provide a mosaic of micro-habitats for the many birds, mammals and insects thriving in their shrubberies, hedges, walls, ponds, herbaceous borders, log piles and compost heaps. Diverse food sources, nesting sites and shelter areas make gardens most attractive sites for wildlife in a highly cultivated agricultural landscape.

The Berkshire, Buckinghamshire and Oxfordshire

Great spotted woodpecker

Swallow

17

Wildlife Trust is promoting a Gardener's Wildlife Challenge to encourage people to improve the biodiversity of their gardens. The Wildlife Trust also works with the Diocese of Oxford to encourage parish groups to conserve the wildlife interest of their local churchyards and cemeteries.

FUTURE LANDSCAPES

While the loss of wildlife and related habitats is widespread, the outlook is not altogether bleak. The efforts of wildlife conservation organisations as described above may prevent any further loss and will hopefully actively increase the habitats available for wildlife.

The other change which may have a positive effect is the increasing interest in organic food. Farming without the use of artificial chemicals will make the agricultural landscape far more attractive to wildlife as farmers work with nature rather than striving to overcome it. Other low-impact farming methods will also help this improvement. In many places already, wide uncultivated verges are left in the fields, these areas acting as a buffer zone between the crops and the hedgerows.

There is an increasing appreciation of the countryside and of environmental issues; this will be the best catalyst to ensure the survival of our native wildlife.

Locations of the Walks

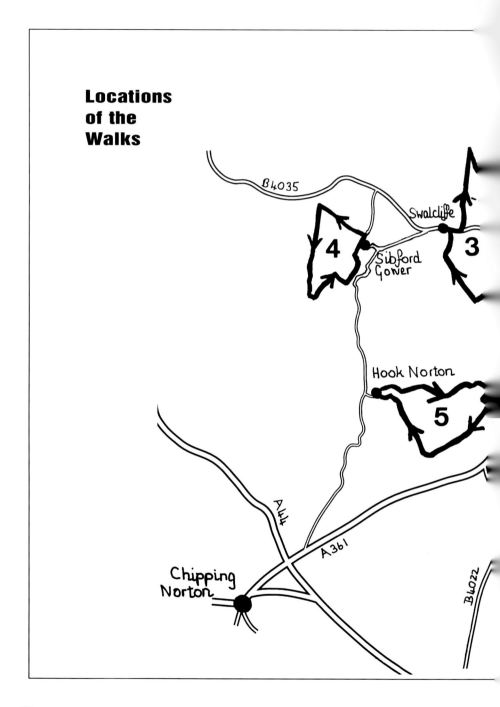

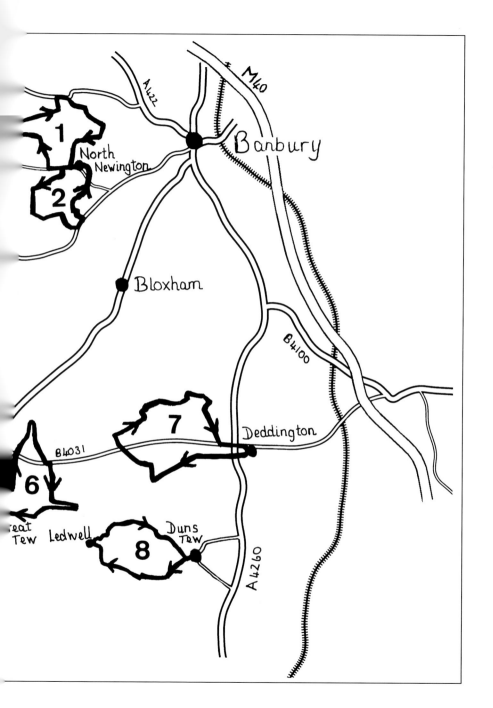

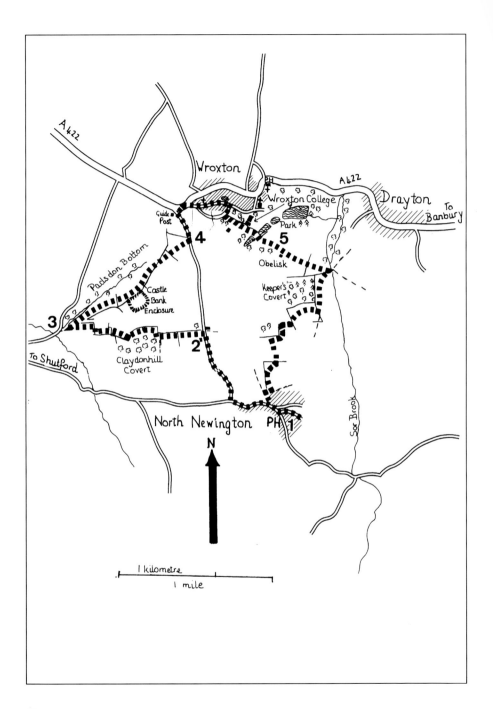

North Newington and Wroxton

4.5 miles 7 km

This route passes through quiet countryside and parkland. The going is easy with just one or two short climbs. There are some muddy places.

1. SP420398

Start in North Newington from the small green opposite the Blinking Owl Inn. With your back to the inn, turn left along the Shutford road. Just outside the village turn right along the road signed to Wroxton. Follow the road uphill for about 1km (0.5 mile) then take the bridleway to the left just past the farm buildings.

North Newington is a small settlement in Broughton parish, its name meaning "new town". The village grew up along the Salt Way, a road linking Droitwich in the west midlands to London. Salt was produced in Droitwich from saline springs, and transported around the country as it was a valuable commodity used to preserve meat for the winter when feed was scarce. The houses along the road past the green were built after inclosure in 1805, the older houses will be seen on Walk 2. There are modern houses too, but most are built using

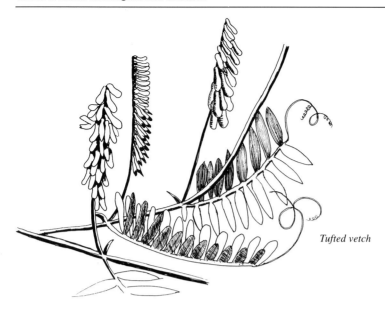

Tufted vetch

materials sympathetic to the local area. The sheltered position of the village in the valley allows good specimens of eucalyptus trees to thrive. They are easy to identify by the silvery grey leaves which hang vertically from the branches. In their native habitat in Australia, this stops the bright sun from striking the leaves directly, thus acting as a means to conserve moisture.

The road to Wroxton was laid out after inclosure in 1805, with wide verges for grazing animals, the road width typically measures about 40 feet from hedge to hedge. A striking plant to look out for in early summer is tufted vetch with deep blue flowers growing in clusters along one side of the stem. This is related to sweet peas and garden peas, all climbing by means of tendrils and all forming seeds in elongated fruit cases or pods.

2. SP412405

Take the path to the left over a stile and along a bridleway with the hedge on the right. Go through a gate into the wood and continue straight on to 100m before the end of the wood. Here go through another

Red admirals on ivy

gate on the right and continue in the same direction as before. Through a metal gate, then carry straight on with the hedge now on the left. Go through a small gate, turning right, then left, and follow the hedge on the right downhill in the same field. Go through a gate, then after 50m turn right through another gate, following the yellow footpath sign.

The bridle way was a more important route in the past and is shown on the 1st edition Ordnance Survey map as a road, probably another laid out during inclosure of the open fields. The fields slope down to the path and are shown as open fields in 1797. A wet flush is visible with rushes and lusher grass, the water coming from a spring further up the slope. There are remnants of ridge and furrow, with the line of the ploughing running down the hillside. This would have aided drainage of the field which probably was wetter in the past as water tables were higher generally before large scale extraction.

In autumn the hedge provides a feast for overwintering redwings, fieldfares, blackbirds and song thrushes. Rose hips, the haws of hawthorn, blackthorn sloes and black bryony berries are converted into body fat, enabling the birds to survive the cold and food scarce winter months. A large ash close to the gateway is festooned with ivy. The greenish-yellow flowers provide nectar eagerly sought by hosts of bees, wasps, flies and red admiral butterflies in October. A cluster of the whitish umbrella-

25

Redwing

shaped fruiting bodies of the parasol fungus may be found at this season emerging through the grass at the field edge.

The name of the woodland, Claydonhill Covert, implies that it was planted or maintained as cover either for pheasants or for foxes, again possibly when inclosure took place. Coppicing was common in coverts to provide dense shelter. Other shrubs often bearing berries were planted for winter food for pheasants. Bluebells grow here in spring and the moist conditions provide an ideal habitat for ferns and mosses, which grow over the ground and fallen timber, giving an almost tropical appearance to the area.

3. SP399406

Following the line of the footpath sign, walk with the hedge to the left, about halfway up the slope. Over a

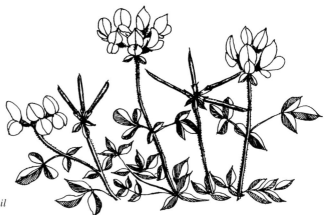

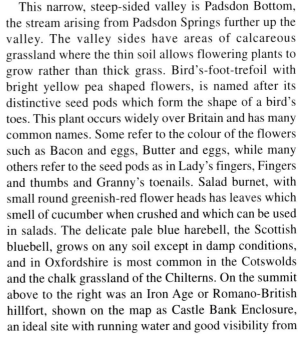

Bird's-foot-trefoil

Harebell

wooden fence, continue along the valley, the path gradually leading up to a stone wall to walk alongside trees and a wire fence. When you reach a stile on the right follow the path diagonally left across the field, and continue in the same direction across the next field to a road.

This narrow, steep-sided valley is Padsdon Bottom, the stream arising from Padsdon Springs further up the valley. The valley sides have areas of calcareous grassland where the thin soil allows flowering plants to grow rather than thick grass. Bird's-foot-trefoil with bright yellow pea shaped flowers, is named after its distinctive seed pods which form the shape of a bird's toes. This plant occurs widely over Britain and has many common names. Some refer to the colour of the flowers such as Bacon and eggs, Butter and eggs, while many others refer to the seed pods as in Lady's fingers, Fingers and thumbs and Granny's toenails. Salad burnet, with small round greenish-red flower heads has leaves which smell of cucumber when crushed and which can be used in salads. The delicate pale blue harebell, the Scottish bluebell, grows on any soil except in damp conditions, and in Oxfordshire is most common in the Cotswolds and the chalk grassland of the Chilterns. On the summit above to the right was an Iron Age or Romano-British hillfort, shown on the map as Castle Bank Enclosure, an ideal site with running water and good visibility from its high vantage point. The slope opposite was common pasture for Wroxton, the parish boundary following the line of the stream, and the land beyond was one of Wroxton's four open fields prior to inclosure in 1804.

4. SP410414

At the road turn left for 300m to a stone sign post with pointing hands showing directions. On the top is an early type of sundial, indicating the months of the year. The post was erected in 1686, at a time when road transport was beginning to improve.

Wroxton guide post

Turn right for 100m then right down Main Street into Wroxton. Past the village duck pond, turn right along a lane to the right of Wroxton College. At a bend take the footpath to the left around the edge of the park. Bear left through a gate and walk with a wire fence to the left for about 150m to a gate on the skyline. Turn left downhill walking parallel to the fence line on the left.

Through the gate follow the path straight on past the lake to a stile. Then walk uphill towards the obelisk on the skyline.

The house was built between 1610-20 by Sir William Pope, founder of Trinity College, Oxford, and incorporated parts of the monastic buildings remaining from St. Mary's Priory, bought by Sir Thomas Pope after its dissolution in 1536. Building continued in the 18th and 19th centuries and it is now a college for American students. The Augustinian priory of St. Mary was founded in the early 13th century and in 1217 there are records of a vineyard. The population of the village dropped drastically during the latter part of the 14th century and by 1391 the priory lands were almost uncultivated because there were so many deaths through epidemics.

The specimen trees you see along this stretch of the walk were planted as part of the landscaping of Wroxton Park in about 1740. Ten years earlier the grounds had been laid out in a symmetric formal

Wroxton village style with avenues of trees and parterres, areas of clipped low hedges often planted in an intricate pattern. The designer was Tilleman Bobart, a pupil of Henry Wise, the gardener of Queen Anne. This must have been planted at the end of this fashion, as already at other places a less formal style was developing which culminated with Capability Brown's "natural" look. The new planting at Wroxton was designed by Sanderson Miller, who later recommended Brown for one of his first commissions. Miller's style was "picturesque" and included buildings such as the Gothic dovecote, a cascade and lakes as well as the natural tree planting. Look out for aspects of the park as you walk.

The obelisk commemorates the visit of Frederick, Prince of Wales in 1739 when he stayed at Wroxton while visiting Banbury races. It was paid for by the Prince in thanks for the hospitality he received here.

As you walk further notice the folly on the skyline amongst the trees.

5. SP419413

Follow the path over this and the next field descending to a small stream in the valley bottom. Just before you cross the stream take a path to the right and cross the field diagonally right to the

Wroxton Park

woodland of Keeper's Covert. At the wood edge continue to the corner, then bear right past a large tree, then diagonally left to the far corner of the wood ahead.

At the track, turn left and return to North Newington, turning left when you reach the road to return to the starting point.

These woods, all named "covert" like Claydonhill Covert seen earlier, were probably planted during the 18th or 19th century by the Broughton estate as at that time North Newington was part of Broughton.

In summer you may see expanses of red poppies flowering in cereal fields. In the past these were common weeds in corn fields, introduced into Britain by early Neolithic settlers along with their seed corn. The development and widespread usage of herbicides in the 1960's wiped out the flowers but viable seeds remained buried in farmland and road sides. Reduction in use of herbicide and the farming practice of set-aside where land is left uncultivated has allowed this poppy to resume its traditional cycle of flowering and seeding. Poppy pollen is important to hive bees as a protein food for their larvae.

As you walk along the track you will pass allotments. These were probably set out at the time of inclosure or later in the 19th century for the use of local people who needed a patch of land to raise vegetables. They would have lost land when the open fields were enclosed as the major land holders gained most from inclosure. For many years allotments were an important feature of village life everywhere but now tend to be less popular due to the variety of food available in supermarkets and lack of time as people work further from their homes.

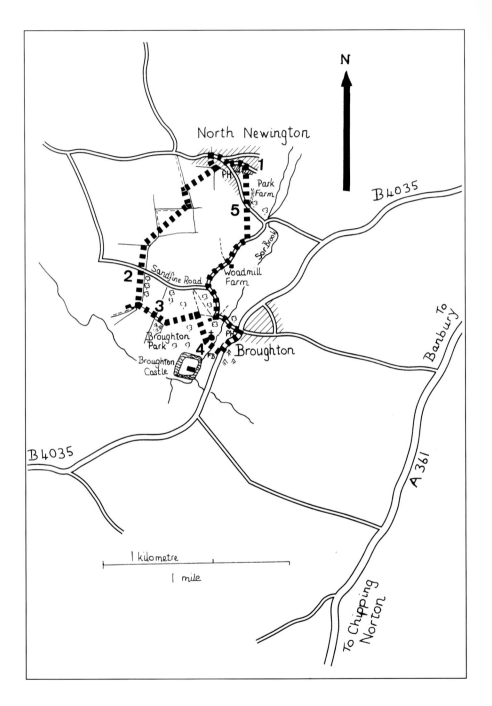

North Newington

Park Farm

B4035

Sor Brook

Woadmill Farm

Sandfine Road

Broughton Park

Broughton Castle

Broughton

To Banbury

B4035

A 361

To Chipping Norton

1 kilometre

1 mile

N

North Newington and Broughton

3 miles   5 km

This is a short pleasant walk along well maintained paths through fields to Broughton Castle and church, returning along quiet lanes.

1. SP420398

Starting outside the Blinking Owl pub, walk west past the Manor House. At the water pump, turn left and walk along The Pound track. At the top of the slope, 20m past the last cottage on the right, take the footpath to the right, up a bank and through the hedge into a field. Take the path diagonally right across the field. At the hedge go left, then at the corner of the field cross a ditch into the next field and follow the permissive path to the right round the edge of the field to a gate at the opposite corner. Here take the path through a gate, and turn left along the hedge to another gate. Through this, keep the hedge on your left and walk to the road.

The road through North Newington was a "saltway" which was an Anglo Saxon and medieval route used for transporting salt from Droitwich to places scattered all over the country. It is thought that this particular route may have eventually led to Princes Risborough in Buckinghamshire. The salt was obtained from naturally occurring saline springs in the Droitwich area of Worcestershire; similar springs are situated in Cheshire. Salt was an important commodity in the past as it was the only way to preserve meat and fish before the days of refrigeration.

The name Newington meant "new settlement" over a thousand years ago, the North element distinguishing it from another "new" settlement to the south. From the field path, the present day modern buildings are visible on the hillside to the far left as you turn to look at the view. The oldest buildings are situated in the sheltered valley and later development spread along the road from the Green after enclosure in 1805.

Along the line of the footpath in many of these fields when sown with oil seed rape or other arable crop, notice the variety of annual "weeds" growing where the ground is uncultivated. Blue field speedwell, yellow field pansy, pink common mallow and common hemp nettle are some of the plants that would probably be eliminated by the spraying of herbicide tolerant genetically modified rape. The resultant decrease in plant diversity would be likely to lead to a decline in insects which depend on such plants for food and shelter.

Agrimony

To the right are the distant hills of the northern Cotswolds. Closer is an attractive landscape of undulating countryside of small woodlands and medium sized arable or pasture fields, bounded by hedgerows.

2. SP412389

Cross the road and take the track which leads through a metal gate. Follow this alongside a woodland strip and then down to a barn. At the barn turn left and walk to the stile ahead.

The road is called Sandfine Road and is an old track which, from the 1797 map of Oxfordshire, appears to have been hedged on one side only. Today the old hedge and bank is

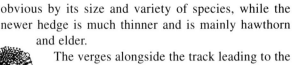

obvious by its size and variety of species, while the newer hedge is much thinner and is mainly hawthorn and elder. The verges alongside the track leading to the barn indicate how uncultivated patches in this area would have looked in the past. It has a good collection of wildflowers; reddish-purple hardheads and greater knapweed, pale blue field scabious, yellow agrimony, bird's-foot-trefoil and creeping cinquefoil. Several of these have been used in herbal medicines; agrimony to stop bleeding, field scabious to treat scabies and sores and cinquefoil to reduce inflammation including toothache. The name of this latter plant is French for "five leaves", describing its five leaflets, whilst its Latin name of *Potentilla reptans* refers to both its medicinal properties and the prolific runners, which give the plant a bad reputation as a fast spreading weed in gardens and allotments.

Field scabious

3. SP413385

Over the stile you enter Broughton Park. Carry straight on to the edge of a small woodland. Here bear diagonally left for about 200m across grassland. At a line of sycamores, turn right down to the church.

The Park was created in the 18th century but by 1880 was reduced to 22 acres, less than half the original area. It contains marks of earlier landscapes with traces of lanes and field boundaries, pillow mounds – artificial burrows for rabbits, quarries and possibly dwellings. This park was a replacement for an earlier deer park and rabbit warren. This land was ploughed in 1674, some decades after 500 acres of the parish were laid down to sheep and cattle pasture when Sir Richard Fiennes inclosed the arable land between 1589 and 1607.

The castle is really a fortified manor house and much of it dates back to the original house and moat built in about 1300 by Sir John de Broughton. In 1377 it was bought by William of Wykeham who founded New College, Oxford, and in 1448 it was linked through

marriage to the Fiennes family in whose hands it still *Broughton Castle* remains. The house was reconstructed into a Tudor mansion during the 16th century which is what is apparent externally today. During the Civil War, this was a Parliamentarian stronghold, besieged after the battle of Edgehill by the Royalists and briefly occupied. In recent years restoration has taken place with aid from English Heritage. Its most recent claim to fame is as a setting for the filming of part of "Shakespeare in Love" which coincidentally starred a member of the Fiennes family. To visit the Castle phone 01295 262624 for opening times.

4. SP419383

·**At the church go through the gate into the churchyard, walk past the church and over a stone footbridge, continuing to the road. Here turn left and walk to the crossroads. Turn left beside the pub, the Saye and Sele Arms, and walk down the lane, past the Park and Castle entrance and continue uphill. At a junction take the right hand fork and continue past Woadmill Farm, and a track leading to sewage works on the right. The verge widens and at this point**

look out for a path to the left leading diagonally right across the field.

The parish church of St. Mary dates from the 14th century and contains tombs and memorials of the Fiennes family. In early summer the churchyard grassland is covered with the white flowers of burnet saxifrage. Its name reflects the two plants it resembles; the basal leaves are very similar to those of salad burnet whilst the traditional belief that it could cure kidney and bladder stones relates it to the saxifrages. In fact the plant belongs to the carrot or *Umbelliferae*, its flowerhead being like a miniature form of cow parsley and hogweed.

The stream crossed by the stone bridge is the Sor Brook and you will see its route again a little further on. The brook feeds the moat and is one of the three streams in the parish which led to development of fulling, dyeing and papermaking in the parish during the 17th century, trades all dependent on a good supply of running water (see Introduction).

Burnet saxifrage

Notice the almshouses and associated well house across the road from the pub by the crossroads. They were built in 1859 in a Gothic style from the local ironstone.

As you walk along the lane, look for the line of willows and poplars along the valley bottom, following the line of the Sor Brook. Both these trees like damp conditions and their presence usually marks a water

Broughton almshouses

course where they are often planted to stabilise the *Cottage in Broughton* banks. These particular willows are young and so have not yet been pollarded, the usual management for older trees to produce new growth and prevent the tree from cracking under its own weight and dying. Crack willow was an important timber used around farms in the past. The pale light wood can be split into thin flexible strips and its pliancy also means that it is resistant to shocks such as those produced by a cricket ball. Poles from pollarded willows were used for making gate hurdles, handles for implements such as scythes, and for use in the framework of laid hedges. A different species, osier willow, can be grown as a coppice tree with shoots harvested after about two years growth. These long flexible "rods" were and still are used for baskets. Different colours are produced by peeling off the bark to produce white rods, or boiling before peeling to produce buff coloured rods. Brown canes have the bark left in situ while green rods are cut in the growing season. Crack willow can also be woven but is not as good for this as osier. A modern use for willow, because

of its fast growth rate, is for use as a renewable fuel for domestic heating.

At Woadmill Farm, pause for a moment to look over the wall at the garden. Many of the plants to be seen are cultivated forms of wild herbs or medicinal plants, which can also often tolerate dry conditions such as found on this rather stony soil. Sneezewort, with double white button shaped flowers was used to make snuff, while borage with blue flowers was used for coughs and treatment of depression. The large pleated leaves of lady's mantle collect dew which early alchemists thought could be used in the conversion of base metals into gold – hence its botanical name of alchemilla. The wild version of the plant may be seen on Walk 5.

The name of Woadmill Farm refers to the woad grown here in the 19th century which was milled by horse power to provide a dark blue dye which was likely to be used locally. The leaves were crushed in the mill and the pulp made into balls which were put to dry. This allowed fermentation to take place within the balls. This process was repeated twice more, when the fully

Sneezewort

Lady's mantle

39

Little owl

fermented and dried pulp was sent off to the dyer. The plant was first recorded in Oxfordshire by a botanist in 1841 near North Newington where it had been cultivated – it may have been here. Today, woad is one of a number of "new" crops cultivated again as an alternative to plentiful food crops. As a dye or ink it has the benefit of being environmentally friendly, another bonus which will hopefully increase its use.

5. SP422395

Over the stile at the end of the path, cross the road with care and go through the gate of Park Farm opposite. Bear slightly left across the grass and walk towards the houses and wall at the far end of the field. Go over the stile alongside the wall and straight on to the road. Here turn left and return along the lane to the starting point.

The large field crossed here has traces of a former lane and possibly buildings, all of which had disappeared before enclosure in 1805. The farm is called Park Farm and was originally the site of a medieval manor house, described in 1852 as "an ancient manor called St. John's in the Wood". The circular building is a dove cot.

A stag headed oak near the farm is a good example of how an aging oak can withstand damage and decay over the years and still survive for may more years. The tree may provide a perch or nest site for the greyish-brown little owl. This bird, which was introduced from the Netherlands in the late 19th century, may also nest in old buildings, the crown of pollarded willows or even rabbit burrows. Formerly persecuted as a predator of game chicks, it has been shown to mainly feed on worms, slugs, larger insects and small rodents.

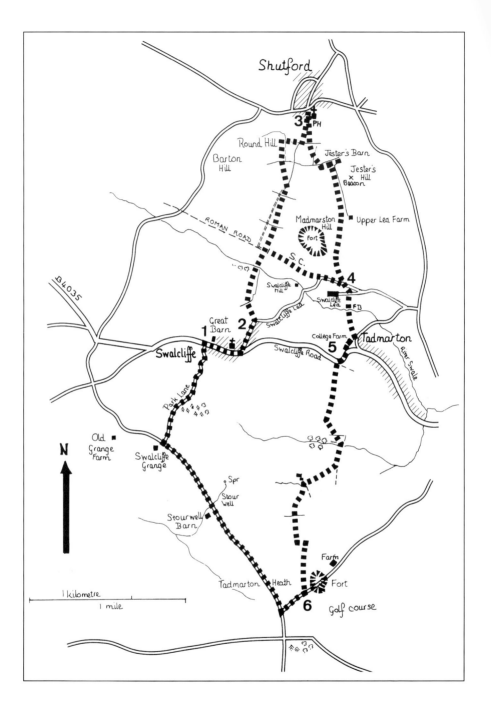

Shutford

3 PH

Round Hill

Barton Hill

Jester's Barn

Jester's Hill Beacon ×

ROMAN ROAD

Madmarston Hill Fort

Upper Lea Farm

S.C.

Swalcliffe Hill

4

B4035

Swalcliffe Lea

Swalcliffe Lea

FB

Great Barn

2

College Farm

5

Tadmarton

1

Swalcliffe

Swalcliffe Road

River Swale

Park Lane

N

Old Grange Farm

Swalcliffe Grange

Spr

Stour Well

Stourwell Barn

Tadmarton Heath

Farm

Fort

6

Golf course

1 kilometre

1 mile

Swalcliffe and Tadmarton

6.5 miles   11 km

Short cut 5.0 miles   8.5 km

This route crosses a Roman road and passes two Iron Age hill forts in pleasant undulating countryside. It is a varied walk on mainly easy tracks with good views.

1. SP377379

Start from the Swalcliffe Great Barn, turning left from the car park along the road past the church. After 400m take the road to the left, Green Lane, signed to Swalcliffe Lea. At the bottom of the hill take the bridleway left to Shutford.

Swalcliffe Great Barn

The Barn dates from the late 15th century and is one of the best examples in the country. It was probably a Manorial barn, storing produce from the estates of New College, Oxford. It still has the original roof timbers and trusses and is roofed with stone tiles. Oxfordshire Museum's collection of agricultural and trade vehicles is now housed here. The Barn is open on Sundays from Easter to October from 2pm-5pm and Bank Holiday Mondays.

Look at the wall alongside the road. Four types of plant grow here which are examples of stages of evolution in the plant kingdom. Most primitive are the yellow, white and green lichens, with the greyish moss slightly more advanced. Dull green, spore bearing polypody fern, growing high on the wall, evolved earlier than seed bearing plants, here represented by yellow stone crop.

The Church of St. Peter and Paul has Saxon walls in the nave and there are still traces of wall paintings. It is

Red valerian

well worth pausing for a visit. Red valerian grows on the walls of the churchyard. This plant was introduced from the Mediterranean during the 16th century and has spread throughout the country, growing on cliff faces, dry banks and old walls. It prefers poor, well-drained, limy soil and is frequently seen in this part of Oxfordshire. The churchyard is a good example of a compromise between neatness and wildlife conservation. In spring and early summer, areas of uncut flowery grassland are left around the ancient graves, contrasting with the regularly mown approaches to the church and the more recent graves.

As you walk through the village notice how many of the older house have steep pitched roofs. This steep pitch indicates houses that were thatched in the past; now just a few remain today. The angle of the roof allowed water to run off quickly.

Just before you reach the bridleway, notice the site of a pond on the left, encircled with willows, which are only found in damp places. Look back to see the old part of the village on the dry ridge. This topography must be the feature giving rise to the name of the village, which comes from the Old English *clif* , one meaning of which is a hill slope. The other part of the name refers to swallows.

2. SP381381

Follow the bridleway round the side of the hill. At the junction of tracks continue in the same general direction, over a small stream to a junction with another track.

For a SHORT CUT turn right to follow the bridleway for about 1km (0.5 mile) to rejoin the main walk at Point 4.

Here turn left for a short distance, pass through a gate, then after 50m take the bridleway on the right, walking with a hedge on your left for about 600m.

Pass through a gate in a hedge and continue ahead for about 75m. Turn left through a gate and walk diagonally right to a gate in a fence at the base of

Round Hill. Continue through the gate in the same direction keeping close to the hedge on the right. Shortly before the end of the field turn right through a gate. Walk downhill close to a wooden fence on the left and after 150m turn left through a gate into a pasture with scattered trees. Walk close to the left edge of this field to a metal gate. Through the gate, take a path downhill into Shutford.

As the track rises there are good views over the nearby countryside. Behind you can see the villages of Swalcliffe and Tadmarton on the ridge and in front, tree covered Barton Hill and the obvious Round Hill. A little further on Madmarston Hill can be seen; later you will be able to see traces of the hill fort situated on its summit. This landscape of distinct hummocky hills was formed by the action of erosion of the Upper Lias clay, capped with limestone (see Introduction).

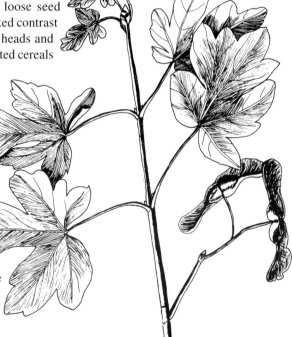

Field maple

The edges of the bridleway contain many different grasses, their loose seed heads and pliable stems a marked contrast to the highly bred dense seed heads and strong stiff stalks of the cultivated cereals growing in the fields.

The small stream is marked by a line of trees and areas of wild flowers. Just beyond this, the verge on the left has been left uncultivated, instead a variety of young trees have been planted. Seeds and fruits of cherry, field maple, ash, beech and oak will sustain birds and small mammals. The long grass and flowers such as St. John's-wort, common vetch and wood avens provide nectar and shelter for insects.

At the junction of tracks, the short section of track followed before continuing through the fields to Shutford is a Roman road which led from Droitwich to a settlement near present day Swalcliffe Lea. This covered about 50 acres with many buildings and possibly a furnace for extracting iron from the local stone. It is thought that the settlement was destroyed by fire in the second century AD then reoccupied about 100 years later until the end of the Roman period. In medieval times the area was used as a quarry, making use of the remains of the Roman buildings.

3. SP386400

After exploring the village, retrace your steps to the metal gate, this time following the left hand path across the field to a stile in the hedge. Over the stile, continue across a cultivated field to a gap in the hedge. Here turn left uphill towards a barn, then turn right following the track along the side of the hill.

St. Martin's and the George and Dragon, Shutford

The track then leads round Upper Lea Farm, bearing to the right of the barn, following markers. Through the gate turn right through the orchard, then at the bottom corner through the next gate, follow the path diagonally left across the field to a lane.

Shutford is the northernmost village in Swalcliffe parish and the path just walked is still the most direct route between the two settlements. The church yard of St. Martins, like that at Swalcliffe, has achieved a balance between wildlife conservation and tidiness. In early summer pink vetch, blue speedwell, yellow hawkbit and orange hawkweed grow alongside the path. The last two are both members of the dandelion family which are numerous and notoriously difficult to identify. However the orange hawkweed is more obvious both by its colour and by the clusters of flowers and buds giving rise to its common name of fox-and-cubs. This plant originates in central Europe and has been introduced into several churchyards in Oxfordshire. The irregular pattern of the ironstone buildings developed during its industrial phase in the 18th and 19th centuries when Shutford was one of the local centres for weavers making plush, a fabric similar to velvet used in liveries and upholstery (see Introduction).

Orange hawkweed

Jester's Barn at the foot of Jester's Hill shows clearly the large doorways for carts and also the covered area between them where hand threshing would have taken place during the winter months before the use of machinery. The corn was stored in sheaves until there was time to separate the grain from the chaff. Using flails to beat the corn, the draught through the doorways helped to blow away the lighter chaff leaving the grain to fall to the ground. Many such barns have fallen into disuse, but are now often preserved by conversion into dwellings. Whilst retaining vernacular buildings in the landscape, this can have a downside for wildlife as buildings like these provide nesting places for barn owls and swallows. Perhaps planning consent should include suitable provision for these birds so that their presence is not lost.

On the hill top is a beacon, one of a chain built across England in 1988 to commemorate the defeat of the Spanish Armada in 1588.

As you walk notice the rough ground on the hill ahead to the right. This marks the remains of the Madmarston Camp with its ditch and embankment. This was occupied during the Iron Age from the 2nd century BC to the 1st century AD with a brief reoccupation around 350A.D. The camp is on the highest part of the hill with a level area possibly for stacking corn or for cattle. Unfortunately most of the hill was ploughed before the site could be designated as a scheduled ancient monument. Sites such as this that are protected often retain unimproved grassland or scrub, a valuable wildlife habitat.

Upper Lea Farm is shown on a map of Oxfordshire made in 1797 with cultivated land sloping up to the hill just walked past and down to present day Swalcliffe Lea. Much of the land in the valley here and reaching up to Swalcliffe was pasture and therefore not ploughed. In contrast, although the orchard which you walk through contains old fruit trees, it overlies previously cultivated land as the ridge and furrow testifies. In early summer notice how the buttercups highlight the ridges.

4. SP390385

(SHORT CUT: To re-join the main trail here turn right onto a footpath leading to a hedge.)

Cross the lane and carry on to the hedge. Continue across the drive through the next hedge and follow the field edge with the hedge to your right. The path leads downhill then between two large ponds. Turn right over a footbridge over the small River Swale and then carry straight on uphill. Look behind to see

Swalcliffe Lea. Over a stile walk diagonally left to the road. Turn right up the rough track past houses to the main road.

The lane you cross is another part of the Roman road. This area was not only a Romano- British site but in the Middle Ages was also a settlement called The Lea with 38 taxable people in 1377. It was still described as a village in the 1660's but fifty years later had declined and houses were in ruins. The cause of this decline seems to have been inclosure when much of the village was abandoned around 1570. Lower Lea Farm still remains today.

The stream and ponds lie on clay which forms a band along the foot of the hills. Clay is impermeable so water drains through porous ironstone or limestone to emerge where it meets the clay. The fast flowing stream was ideal for water mills; there was a fulling mill upstream from here before the 16th century. The corn mill at Swalcliffe Lea was still working in 1851.

The verge along the track leading to the main road contains pink rest harrow and black medick, a member of the clover family with small yellow flowers, both meadow plants. One of the houses, mostly redeveloped farm buildings, is called The Old Rickyard, which is a reminder of the past importance of hay storage for winter feed in ricks or haystacks. Now most grass is kept as silage. Grass can be cut green at its best growth, stored in airtight conditions where it partially ferments, often now with the aid of chemicals, thus preserving it. This is far less labour intensive than hay making which relies on dry weather at the right time, and turning to ensure all the grass is properly dried. However, hay making seems to be making a return to the countryside, perhaps helped by the increasing interest in horses.

5. SP390379

At the main road carry on uphill in the same direction. Where the road bends sharply right go through a gate and take the bridleway straight on signed South Newington. Walk straight on across the

field. At the next gate, head diagonally left downhill towards the trees. Through another gate, the path goes between a rocky outcrop, then reaches the trees which surround a stream. Continue uphill through a similar outcrop. Bear left off the obvious track and aim towards a single ash tree on the hillside and continue uphill towards the barns. Go left through the gate and follow the track. Through another gate continue along the track bearing slightly left. Where the track leads left to a farm, carry straight on with the fence on your right to reach the road.

Tadmarton is another settlement situated on the dry high ground. Records of agriculture here go back to 956AD when open strip fields were already established.

Salad burnet

By 1086 the land was held by Abingdon Abbey with a tenant holding part of it. Each estate had meadow, pasture and a watermill. The land remained as open fields in various arrangements of two and later four fields until inclosure in 1776.

There are wide views over the fields and hills in this section of the walk. A landmark to the left is the spire of Bloxham church. A local legend about the building of this church says that one particular mason was famed for his craftsmanship, until one day he fell. His load of stones became Crouch Hill outside Banbury and the mason disappeared in a cloud of sulphur, the other builders realising that he was the Devil!

The stony holloway is an oasis of wild flowers in an agricultural landscape. Salad burnett can be found here, with small dark red tight flower heads, and mouse-eared hawkweed, another member of the dandelion family with small pale lemon flowers, tinged with red underneath the petals. Yellow bird's-foot-trefoil is a member of the pea family and produces seed pods arranged in a fan of three or four, resembling a bird's foot. A more uncommon plant is meadow saxifrage; like the others found here it is lime tolerant. The poor soil suppresses vigourous grasses and coarse plants which would smother these more delicate plants in a deeper, richer soil. Similar plants can be found as you walk uphill, but

51

notice how growth here is more lush indicating that the soil is deeper and that the holloway is more shaded.

Look to your left as you walk towards the barns and beyond them. Notice how the steep slopes are unsuitable for large scale modern arable farming, the land being used for grazing instead, with some areas looking quite rough and scrubby. This will make a marked contrast to the landscape you will see on your way back to Swalcliffe. If you look closely, you will see that in the past this land has been cultivated. There are traces of ridge and furrow leading down the slopes, showing that more simple techniques could cope with the difficult terrain. The land here may have been pasture since the late 18th century as by then much of the parish was under grass for grazing or hay-making.

Broom

As you approach the road, you will pass an area of trees and gorse and rough grass. This is Tadmarton Heath Camp, another Iron Age hill fort which encloses five acres in a ring of two banks and ditches, bisected by the road. The plants which grow here like yellow flowering gorse and broom, foxgloves and bracken indicate the acid nature of the soil, a great difference to the limestone seen by the stream. This was another area of common land in the parish where local people had common rights to cut furze or gorse. The old or dead stems were used as kindling and fuel, particularly for bread making because of the heat it generates, and the younger growth for animal feed. The cutting of furze was often strictly regulated, demonstrating its importance for the local people.

6. SP387356

At the road turn right and walk with care to the next junction where you take the minor road to the right. Continue downhill, past a house and well in the valley bottom. Continue slightly uphill until the road reaches a junction at Swalcliffe Grange. Turn right here and follow Park Lane back to Swalcliffe. At the main road cross with care to return to the Barn.

The road here is an ancient one, originating as a prehistoric track from the Cotswolds. Notice the slight bump in the surface to the left where the remains of the fort lie. By the 19th century it was a drove road, used by herdsmen taking their flocks across country. Wherever possible they would avoid paying tolls and this road was reputed to cover 100 miles without going through a toll gate. The main road through Swalcliffe and Tadmarton was a turnpike between 1781 and 1872 with regular toll houses where dues were collected which paid for upkeep and was income for shareholders in the turnpike trust.

More evidence of heathland can be seen across the road on the golf course, but a little further along the road, the verge is full of meadow cranesbill which has a profusion of blue flowers in summer. This is usually abundant on limestone soil so its presence here might mark the transition from acid heathy soil to limestone. Alternatively the road might have been made up with limestone chippings in the past which have altered the local soil chemistry.

The minor road you follow downhill is another ancient road which eventually links with Ditchedge Lane (see Walk 4 Sibford Gower). It passed through another settlement, Holwell Grange, belonging to the Cistercian Abbey of Bruern, and which disappeared at about the same time as The Lea. On the map this is now marked by Old Grange farm.

Notice the wide expanse of open arable fields, a great contrast to the grazing land seen earlier. In the distance to the left is the ridge followed by Ditchedge Lane and beyond that the Cotswolds.

The house is called Stourwell Barn, and the remains of Stour Well can still be seen where a spring enters the old stone trough on the right.

The wood was part of Swalcliffe Park which was probably created in 1772 when Swalcliffe was enclosed and the lord of the manor, William Wykeham was allotted 579 acres. The house, the seat of the Wykeham family, was probably rebuilt at about the same time and altered again in the 19th century. It is now a school.

53

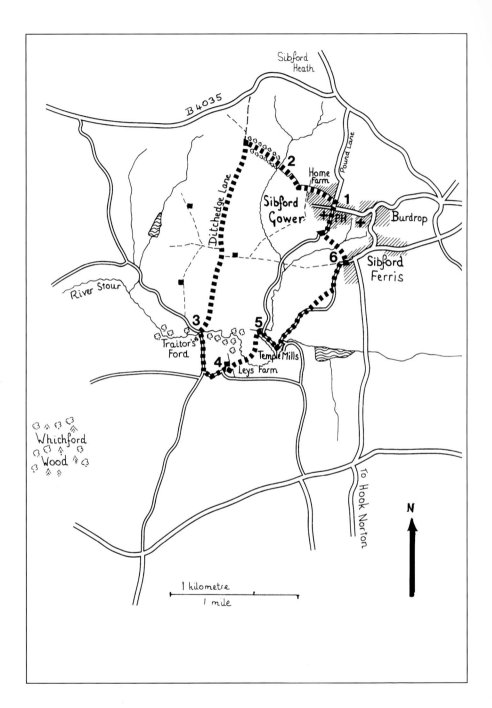

Sibford Gower and Sibford Ferris

4.5 miles   7 km

A pleasant walk with wide views and attractive landscapes. There are some short steepish climbs and it can be very muddy in several places.

1. SP352379

From the crossroads in Sibford Gower, take Pound Lane uphill (signed Epwell and Shipton on Stour). After 50 metres take the bridleway to the left along Backside Lane. Continue straight on past Home Farm, through a gateway, down the lane and through another gate. Continue alongside a spring to the right of the hedge downhill to reach a stream at the bottom.

Sibford Gower was originally a township in the ancient parish of Swalcliffe, but became a separate parish, both civil and ecclesiastical, in the 19th century. Sibford means Sibba's ford, possibly the name of one of the first Saxon settlers here. Gower was taken from Goher, the name of the 13th century lords of the manor. In 1086 there were two manors listed here in the Domesday Book, both appearing to be in a run down state compared with cultivation levels prior to the

Norman Conquest. This is likely to be a result of rebellions after the invasion.

Many houses, built of local stone and with thatched roofs, date from the 17th century. There are some later additions, some of which are walked past in Backside Lane. Many of these 20th century additions are built in a vernacular style of materials which blend well with the older buildings.

As you follow the path downhill, notice that it mostly a well defined holloway. The path has sunk below the level of the surrounding land, worn away over centuries of use by the passage of feet and by water erosion. A map of Oxfordshire made in 1797 shows this route to be equivalent in importance to others which are roads today. It is not known why some routes declined while others remained important.

About halfway down the hill, at the foot of a large ash tree, water bubbles out of the ground from one of the numerous springs in the area. Springs are formed where limestone meets impermeable clay, so forcing the water held in the porous rock to emerge.

The view to the right extends to Sibford Heath on the skyline. Originally this area would have been rough grass, bracken and gorse used for grazing and fuel collection; it is now agricultural land.

Wood avens

2. SP347383

Go through the gate and cross the stream. Continue in the same direction as before, climbing uphill between hedges. At the junction with another track, turn left. Follow this track for 2.5km (1.5 mile) until it descends and you reach the road.

As you walk uphill it is easier to see that this is an old route. The path is actually quite wide but the encroaching scrub make it appear much narrower. The path can be very muddy but notice where conditions underfoot change; this marks the transition from clay to limestone at the springline.

Yellow flowered wood avens can be found on the hedge banks. "Avens" probably refers to the bristly seeds

Shaggy parasol

and is derived from the Latin word *avena* describing an awned oat seed. An alternative name is Herb Bennet, a corruption of the medieval name of herba benedicta or blessed herb. In the past it was widely used as a medicinal herb, efficacious perhaps because it contains the volatile oil eugenol. Its aromatic root was used to flavour ale. In autumn, look on the bank for the brownish umbrella shaped mushrooms of the shaggy parasol.

The track at the top of the hill which you follow for a distance marks the county boundary between Oxfordshire and Warwickshire. This ancient route, called Ditchedge Lane, runs between Sibford Heath and Rollright, either as a path as here or as a road. It may be a branch of the so-called Jurassic Way between Somerset to Lincolnshire which follows the crest of the north Oxfordshire uplands. Whatever its roots, this track was in existence by the 10th century. The track is now part of another modern long distance route. You will notice signs for the Macmillan Way, devised as a walk to raise sponsorship and awareness of the work of the Macmillan nurses in caring for terminally ill cancer patients and their families.

There are large areas of bracken along the track. In the past this was used as bedding for farm animals. However now that it is no longer used in this way and mowing has long since stopped, bracken has invaded grazing land and is a nuisance in many places. It is difficult to eradicate as it spreads by underground rhizomes (stems). It can be poisonous to browsing animals and its spores are suspected of causing human cancer if inhaled in large amounts.

Nettles also grow in numbers along the track. This indicates that in the past the route was used to drive herds or flocks of animals. Their dung has enriched the soil, so favouring the growth of nettles. The nutrients are recycled as the decomposing nettle leaves return them to the soil.

The hedge to the right is an example of an old coppice hedge. This gives thick tall cover and a food store for our resident thrushes and their winter-visiting Scandinavian cousins, redwing and fieldfare. Such coppice management should be carried out on a rotation ensuring that at all times some mature lengths of hedgerow are available to these timid birds.

There are wide views from this ridge path. To the left is the valley you have just walked through but to the right long views over Warwickshire can be seen across the River Stour valley towards Moreton-in-Marsh. The

Skylark

large wood is Whichford Wood, an old woodland. On the far skyline, is Brailes Hill topped by a tree clump. Further along, pause to look to the right at an uncultivated and unsprayed field which in summer is full of flowers. White ox-eye daisies, bright yellow meadow vetchling and the pink flowers of black knapweed or hardhead attract many insects. Skylarks can be seen and heard here as well, nesting in the grass. Later in the year, the seed heads will attract flocks of several types of finch. This richness is a contrast to the majority of fields seen everywhere in the countryside today.

3. SP337374

Turn left along the road, crossing the River Stour by ford or bridge. Continue uphill to the junction and turn left. Follow this road downhill, crossing a bridge at the bottom then climb until you reach a footpath sign to the left to Leys Farm.

Traitor's Ford is medieval and is an ideal way to wash the mud off your boots from the earlier part of the walk! On the right as you walk uphill are several disused quarries and also a lime kiln, now hidden by tree growth. Lime was used as a manure or fertiliser in the 18th century also to reduce the acidity of the heathy soil in this area. There are the remains of several kilns hereabouts.

Beyond the trees, the verge on the left is colourful in summer with plant species, some of which prefer a limy soil. Yellow lady's bedstraw has tiny flowers in dense soft spikes while agrimony, again with yellow flowers, has stiffer spikes and larger flowers. This is another plant which was widely used in herbal medicine, recommended for snake bites and "elf-shot" or unaccountable illness in the Middle Ages. Knapweed with pinkish purple flowers and pale blue field scabious can also be seen. Pale coloured red bartsia is sometimes mistaken for heather, but here the soil is too limy for the latter. This plant can attach itself by suckers to take nutrients from the roots of red clover. The clover is weakened and its capacity for nitrogen enrichment of

Ringlet butterfly

the soil is reduced. The poorer soil is colonised by flowering plants which thrive without strong competition from grasses.

Ringlet butterflies seek nectar from these flowers. The "eyes" at the edges of their wings tend to divert attacks by birds away from their vulnerable bodies. In contrast skipper butterflies, also seen here, rely on a fast darting flight to avoid capture. These can be identified by their triangular appearance, very different to the usual butterfly shape.

Further on, pink pea-like flowers of rest harrow can be seen on the verge just before the entrance to Leys Farm. Before the advent of tractors, land invaded by this

Rest harrow

Musk thistle

plant was difficult to plough due to its tangled mass of tough underground stems (rhizomes). The hairy leaves, sticky to the touch, are covered in oil secreting glands.

As you approach the farm, look out for two varieties of thistle in midsummer. Musk thistle has a pleasant almond scent and its reddish-purple, drooping flowerheads give it the alternative local name of nodding thistle. The deep yellow sow-thistle has young tender leaves which may be eaten in a salad or cooked as a vegetable, whereas the leaves of other thistles are unpalatable to grazing animals and humans alike. Both these plants are members of the Compositae or daisy family, the world's most prolific and versatile family of flowering plants. The composite head of florets is one of the most evolutionary advanced in the plant kingdom.

4. SP339360

Follow the path through Leys Farm and then through a gate, and keeping close to a fence on the right descend to the river. Pass through the gate, cross the river and continue to the top of the bank to a stile at the top. Carry on to the top of the hill, following the

Sow-thistle

61

line of the telegraph poles then bear left downhill
eventually reaching the far left corner of the field.
Go through the gate beside the stream and follow
this to the road. Here turn right.

Leys Farm, shown as Hook Norton Ley's on the 1st
Edition Ordnance Survey Map in 1830, is quite
traditional in appearance. The tall building with
a corrugated iron roof may once have been
thatched, as such steep pitched roofs are typical
of old thatch. There are the remnants of an
orchard on the right.

The bank you climb as you
leave the small river valley has an
abundance of wild flowers, most of
which are scarce in this area, showing
that this is old pasture which has not been treated with
herbicides or synthetic fertilizers. Pink flowered thyme
owes its fragrance to the volatile oil, thymol, released
when the plant is crushed. This is an antiseptic, a
property exploited in cultivated types as a component
of medicines used to treat respiratory and oral
complaints. Burnet saxifrage, a member of the carrot *Quaking grass*
family has a misleading name. Burnet refers to the
similarity of its lower leaves to those of salad burnet, a
member of the rose family while saxifrage alludes to its
traditional use in dispersing kidney and bladder stones,
a property also attributed to true saxifrages (see Walk
8). Quaking grass is very typical of old limestone
grasslands and has distinctive heart shaped flower
spikelets which flutter in the breeze.

5. SP344365

**Turn right along the road and continue past Temple
Mills. Take the turning to the left uphill, just past
the garden. Follow this road until it bears sharply
right; here take the footpath which continues straight
on. Follow the path crossing a stile and continuing
across the next field in the same direction. At the road
turn left. At the next bend continue, ignoring the
bridleway to the left. On the outskirts of Sibford**

Ferris take the footpath to the left, signed Circular Walk to Sibford Gower.

Temple Mills has a long history. A watermill on a tributary of the River Stour, it may have been one of the mills recorded in the Domesday Book. It certainly dates from the 12th century when it was given to the Templars, hence its name. In 1338 it passed to the Hospitallers, valued at £1. The Knights Templar and the Knights Hospitaller were religious orders of knights and together were the most important military orders during the Crusades. The Templars were suppressed in 1312 by Phillip IV of France who feared their power. The mill was still working in 1939 but closed after the Second World War.

The stream marks the parish boundary between Sibford Ferris and Hook Norton. The buildings here are a mixture of old and modern. The house is built of local ironstone and limestone, other buildings are of imported bricks and Welsh slate, and the most modern agricultural buildings are made of wood and metal sheeting.

At the top of the hill, on the left, is an example of a barn conversion. Although such conversions are sometimes controversial, they are a means of conserving a traditional part of the rural landscape through finding a new use for a redundant building.

Further along the road and as you enter the field, you

Corn marigold

Corncockle

may be fortunate to discover the yellow flowered corn marigold, also known as gold, and the reddish purple corncockle both flowering in midsummer. These handsome cornfield flowers are now very uncommon in the English countryside due to their virtual eradication by herbicides since the 1950's. They have always been regarded as pernicious weeds; corncockle made bread taste bitter and possibly poisonous, while corn marigold caused straw to rot as it does not dry well. An edict to encourage the destruction of Guilde Weed (corn marigold) was issued by Henry II in the 12th century and in the Boke of Husbandry published in 1523 it was listed as *harmful plant*. In very traditional rural areas on the Continent, such as parts of Umbria in Italy, these plants can still be seen in many corn fields, giving an attractive appearance but an obviously low yield of corn.

Here you may also spot two types of red poppy; one

with a round seed head and the other an elongated seed head. Again disliked as cornfield weeds because their poisonous alkaloids can contaminate a grain harvest, these poppies have largely been suppressed by the use of herbicides. However since the advent of set-aside, whereby some fields are temporarily not cultivated to reduce grain surpluses, poppies are re-appearing due to the longevity of their seeds. They are often also seen when ground is disturbed after many years for example by road building or other construction.

6. SP354373

Take the footpath straight down hill to a gate at the bottom. Go over the stream, then diagonally left. Go over the stile and across the next field in the same direction through two kissing gates to the road. At the road turn right and walk uphill through Sibford Gower to your starting point.

The grassy field has hillocks and hollows – this may be due to the long term effect of the water course in the valley bottom, or the remnants of past quarrying, or even traces of old habitation.

The stream is another branch of the headwaters of the River Stour and is fed by springs arising further up the valley.

As you walk through Sibford Gower you will pass a Friends Meeting House; both Sibfords historically have strong links with Quakers or the Society of Friends, as does Banbury which was prominent nationally as a centre for Quakers during the 17th century. Today there is still a Quaker school in Sibford Ferris.

The 17th century Wykeham Arms, formerly a farm house, commemorates William of Wykeham, Bishop of Winchester, who was Chancellor to Edward III. In the late 14th century he founded New College Oxford and was a person of great influence in this region (see Walk 2).

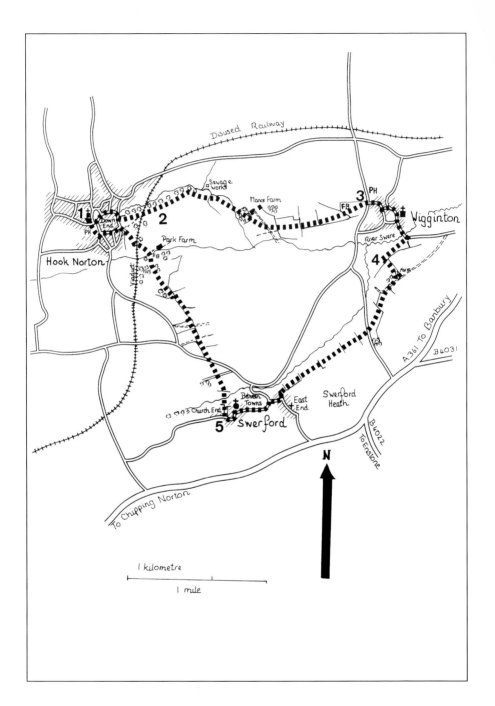

Hook Norton, Swerford and Wigginton

6 miles   10 km

This route leads through three very attractive villages and quiet fields. There are several short steepish climbs and many stiles to negotiate. A low lying area towards the end of the walk may be flooded after heavy rainfall.

1. SP355331

Start by the parish church in Hook Norton. With your back to the church, go left past the Bell Inn. Turn right along Down End for 250m then bear right along Park Hill. Take the footpath signed Swerford and Wigginton to the left uphill through trees. Continue along the edge of a field with a hedge on your left. At the railway embankment, bear left then follow the path between remains of the old bridge to emerge in the open again.

Hook Norton name refers to its earliest inhabitants – "the people at Hocca's hill slope" but between the 14th and 16th century it was known as Hog's Norton when

St. Peter's, Hook Norton

the village was famed for its rusticity. Later it became quite industrialised with a weaving trade, a brewery which still exists and the Brymbo Ironworks which opened in 1896 and worked until 1926 utilising the ironstone quarried locally. The church of St. Peter is worth a visit. It has Anglo-Saxon origins and a Norman chancel with wall paintings of the Zodiac as well as Adam and Eve. As you walk, look out for cottages with long rows of windows which enabled weavers to work in a good light. The disused railway, which you will also see at the end of your walk, was part of the Banbury-Cheltenham line which opened here in 1887 and closed in 1964. Now part of its old route is a nature reserve.

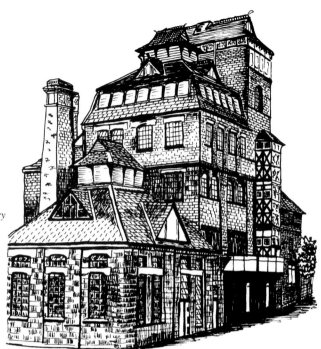

Hook Norton brewery

2. SP362333

Walk along the field edge with a woodland strip on your left. After a while notice the remains of an old linear quarry to the right and a marshy area near a small sewage treatment works on the left. Soon after cross a stile and after 150m turn left to cross a stile and a footbridge. Bear right round the edge of a small wood, then straight on alongside farm buildings. Go right on to a farm track passing the farmhouse on the left. Continue across the field to a gate in the centre of the hedge. Through this, continue straight on across the field to another gateway through a thick hedge. Continue in the same direction with a hedge on the right. Cross a footbridge through a hedge and carry on as before. When the field narrows go through a small gate in the left hedge. Over a stone bridge bear right and walk up hill towards a house in the far left corner of the field to reach the road.

Along the edge of the woodland there is a colourful display of summer flowers typical of verges and uncultivated places. Musk mallow has large pale pink flowers and very divided leaves. Its musky scent gives rise to its name. This is related to the more widespread common mallow with darker pink flowers. Mallows are popular garden plants as are hollyhocks which belong to the same family. Another plant with a garden relation is the yellow and orange toadflax with snapdragon-shaped flowers. The name comes from the resemblance of the narrow leaves to those of flax, which you may see growing in fields further along the route. Its colouring gives rise to another name of "butter and eggs". This plant was originally from southern Europe and is now found on rough ground and waste tips as far north as southern Scotland. It can carry on flowering into November so is a welcome sight amongst the brown stalks of other plants.

In the marshy area are two plants which are characteristic of wet ground. Meadowsweet has frothy cream flowers with an aromatic sweet scent. It has been useful through the ages; to flavour mead and to perfume medieval houses when spread on the floor along with rushes. Its most important derivative is salicylic acid

Musk mallow

Butterbur

which was distilled both from this and willow at the end of the 19th century. This led to the production of aspirin, which was named after the old botanical name for meadowsweet of *Spirea*. The other plant to look for is butterbur which has large rhubarb-like leaves and chunky spikes of pink flowers in early spring before the leaves are up. These flexible leaves were used to wrap butter and keep it cool while their size makes them ideal sun shades or umbrellas. Their Latin name *Petasites* is derived from the Greek for a broad-brimmed felt hat.

As you cross the wooden footbridge over the stream you may be lucky enough to glimpse a grass snake swimming in the water. The olive-green colouration with a white or yellow collar below the head clearly distinguishes this non-poisonous snake from the rarer adder with its black indented stripe along its back. Grassnakes frequent wetlands and watercourses, feeding on toads, small frogs, fish and even tadpoles, whilst adders are found in drier places and feed on small mammals and fledgling birds.

Past the thick hedge, which marks the parish boundary between Hook Norton and Wigginton, as you walk through the flat fields towards Wigginton, notice the tall clumps of grass in the right hand border. This is tufted hair grass or tussock grass which has coarse leaves with saw-like edges which are unpalatable to farm stock. As these fields are mown for hay, this would be an unwelcome addition.

As you walk through these fields notice the ridges and furrows (see Introduction), which can be clearly seen as you climb the hill and pause to look back. You can see how the patterns of ridges change direction, those up the hillside at right angles to those below. You can see how hedges cross these patterns, indicating that the hedges were planted long after the formation of the ridge and furrow. Wigginton parish was enclosed in 1796, transforming the open fields into the pattern seen today. The ridge and furrow has remained in this area because the ironstone is close to the surface, so making large scale arable farming unprofitable, leaving the land for pasture and meadow instead.

3. SP387334

At the road, cross with care and continue through Wigginton past the cottages. At the next junction bear left past the Old Rectory and the church. Carry on down hill past an old water mill and over a stone bridge crossing the river at the bottom. Here turn right over a stile and footbridge, then left over another stile and footbridge, then uphill bearing right to the far top corner of the field. Continue for 100m to cross a stile on the left.

Wigginton belonged to Wicga, a Saxon lord who may have owned much land in the area. In 1086, the manor was held by Guy d'Oilley, the younger brother of Robert who was an important man in Oxfordshire. Earlier, there was Roman occupation in this area with possibly a military post as well as a villa. The proximity of water is probably one reason for this, notice the numbers of springs and streams shown on the Ordnance Survey map. Notice also the number of Victorian water pumps along the village streets which brought water to residents more easily than by fetching it from the river. Another use for flowing water is to power the mill at the bottom of the hill. This is a 19th century mill which ground grain into flour. The Welsh slate roof is an unusual feature in the village where many other roofs are thatched.

On the bridge, pause for a moment to look for damsel flies and dragonflies in summer hunting above the River Swere for midges and mosquitoes. Those with dark blue patches on their wings are the males of the banded Agrion damselflies, one of the largest species. They always rest with their wings closed vertically above their body, distinguishing them from the bigger dragonflies which rest with their wings spread. Toads, the major prey of grassnakes may be seen in the bankside vegetation.

Among the many colourful flowers to be seen in midsummer in the damp grassland is greater bird's-foot-trefoil, a larger relation of the common bird's-foot-trefoil. It is only found in this type of habitat in contrast

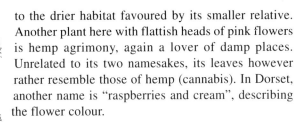

to the drier habitat favoured by its smaller relative. Another plant here with flattish heads of pink flowers is hemp agrimony, again a lover of damp places. Unrelated to its two namesakes, its leaves however rather resemble those of hemp (cannabis). In Dorset, another name is "raspberries and cream", describing the flower colour.

4.SP389328

Immediately cross a second stile and continue uphill. Cross another stile in the fence about 50m from the far left corner. Take the path ahead through young trees down to a yard then turn right down a track. When the track bears right, take a left turning and follow the way-marked path across the next two fields, bearing slightly left in the second, to the road. Cross over and take the path signed to Swerford. Continue across two fields and stiles in the same general direction. At a third field, bear slightly left to the far corner. Pass through a gap in the hedge and walk uphill to the right of another hedge to reach gardens at the back of Swerford.

Hemp agrimony

Carry straight on behind the gardens to a stile on the left between walls. Walk to the road between houses and turn right. At the next junction take the left fork and continue in the same direction past the church and the war memorial. At the footpath sign turn right.

As you climb the hill look across the valley to see more signs of ridge and furrow as well as lynchets, formed to allow cultivation in terraces on steep slopes when agriculture was pushed to its limits prior to the Black Death in the 14th century, when the population was high.

The flat fields between Wigginton and Swerford were open arable fields until 1796. The slopes to the left were Swerford Leys, now called Swerford Heath, but then open land used for grazing. Here you may see a relatively

73

St. Mary's, Swerford

new crop – blue or white flowered flax, used for production of cattle food, and oil which is used in the production of linoleum, now becoming popular again because of its natural ingredients. However, in the Middle Ages flax was grown for its fibrous stalks, used to make linen cloth. This use can often be found reflected in old field names.

Swerford is divided into three sections; East End, where the path reaches the village, Between Towns, and Church End, around the church. **Just before you reach**

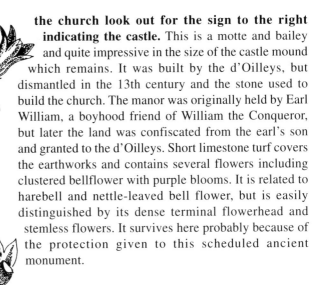

the church look out for the sign to the right indicating the castle. This is a motte and bailey and quite impressive in the size of the castle mound which remains. It was built by the d'Oilleys, but dismantled in the 13th century and the stone used to build the church. The manor was originally held by Earl William, a boyhood friend of William the Conqueror, but later the land was confiscated from the earl's son and granted to the d'Oilleys. Short limestone turf covers the earthworks and contains several flowers including clustered bellflower with purple blooms. It is related to harebell and nettle-leaved bell flower, but is easily distinguished by its dense terminal flowerhead and stemless flowers. It survives here probably because of the protection given to this scheduled ancient monument.

5. SP371311

Follow the footpath along the back of gardens then downhill to cross the stream (River Swere) at the bottom. Go straight on to cross a stile in the hedge, over a footbridge to cross another stile. Then bear left across a field to the next stile. Carry on in the same direction to another stile, then cross the track and through a gate, following the footpath to the road. At the road turn right for about 10m then take the path to the left, signed Hook Norton, and go down a small slope to the field where you turn left. Walk to the right of a hedge for 100m At the track go left. At the end of the hedge carry straight on uphill to reach a farm track.. Turn left for 10m then right on to a grassy path eventually leading downhill. Cross a fence and after 150m look out for a stile to the left and cross this into the next field and continue as before. Over another stile, continue downhill through a young plantation. At the end continue straight on down the field, heading in the general direction of the old viaduct pillars and the way-marked post ahead. Descend a short slope and cross the grass to take the stile left into uncut grass and young trees.

Clustered bellflower

Bear right downhill and cross a marshy area to reach a stream. Cross a footbridge and bear left uphill to climb a stile. Bear left across a small field to a gate. Through the gate, turn left onto a track.

Railway viaduct, Hook Norton

At the road turn left along Park Road, turn right over the bridge and walk up Middle Hill Lane back to the start.

The fields you walk through in this part of the walk are used for horses as paddocks and for hay. This reflects the changes in landscape use as a result of the popularity of horse riding, as fields are split by fences into smaller units.

As you walk down hill towards Hook Norton and Park Farm, look for the small pleated leaves and greenish-yellow small flowers of lady's mantle. This is found in damp grassland and is quite uncommon in this part of Britain. Its garden relation is a bigger plant and came originally from the Carpathian mountains in Eastern Europe. The name comes from the shape of the leaf which resembles a cloak, and "lady" refers, like many other plant names, to Our Lady.

From this slope you can see that this valley is much

wider than would be expected from the size of the stream which flows through it. This may be a valley which was formed by melt water at the end of the Ice Age (see Introduction).

The tall stone piers amongst the trees are the remains of the viaduct which carried the railway line over the valley. They were left when the line was closed and the rest of the track removed.

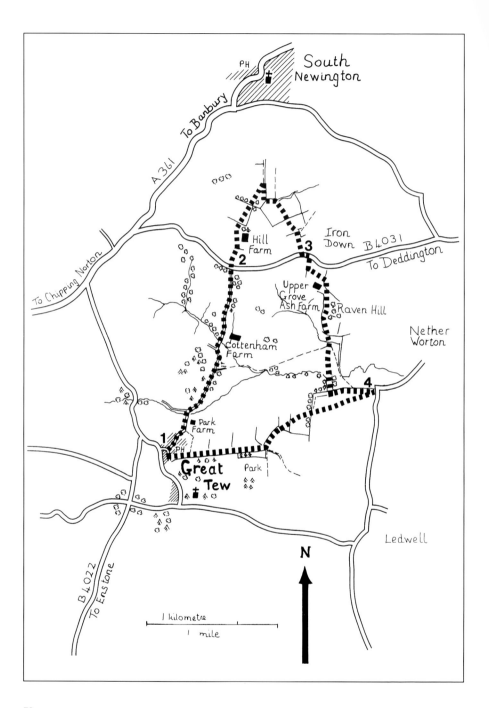

South Newington

PH

To Banbury

A 361

To Chipping Norton

Hill Farm

2

3

Iron Down B4031

To Deddington

Upper Grove Ash Farm

Raven Hill

Nether Worton

Cottenham Farm

4

Park Farm

1

PH

Great Tew

Park

Ledwell

B4022

To Enstone

N

1 kilometre

1 mile

Great Tew

6 miles   10 km

This walk explores the designed landscape of Great Tew and beyond, with some good wide views. There are some climbs but generally the going underfoot is good.

1. SP395293

Starting from the public car park, turn left towards the post office, then left again downhill. At the junction of tracks go left along the bridleway past Park Farm. At the next junction of tracks turn right. Ignore a turning to the right at the next junction. After the track curves to the left, bear right at the next junction and continue along the track climbing gradually to the road, past Cottenham Farm.

Great Tew is famed for its unspoiled appearance. The 17th century houses are built of brownish Hornton stone either in blocks or more random smaller stones. Alterations were made to many houses during the 19th century when the village was owned by descendants of Matthew Boulton, one of the leaders of the Industrial Revolution. Some still have their original thatch whilst others have Stonesfield slate roofs. The village is now largely restored, but some years ago it was in a bad state of repair due to lack of estate funds to maintain the cottages.

Apart from the village itself, the landscape around

Great Tew is interesting because of the remnants of John Claudius Loudon's design for a model estate, based on the Scottish farming methods of arable and grass. Loudon, famous mainly for public and municipal landscape design, came to Great Tew in 1808 and attempted to integrate farmland and park into one landscape for the then owner G. F. Stratton. Loudon laid out a new field pattern, regulating the size of fields depending on their situation and halving the number. The existing tenants were dispossessed and the land let to a group of Scottish farmers. New roads linked the fields and farms, following the contours to make easy access for carts. Many exotic trees were planted in the parkland; today these are the most obvious signs of Loudon's work.

Village centre, Great Tew

As you walk along the track leading away from the village, you cannot help but notice fine specimens of bluish and green cedars. Since these trees were probably planted when this ornamental park was created in the early 19th century, they are likely to be Cedars of Lebanon as the other two species, Atlas and Deodar were not introduced to England until later in the 19th century. Other notable trees include Chile pines, more commonly known as monkey-puzzle trees, giant sequoias and

Monkey-puzzle tree

redwoods with their soft red bark. These last two come from California where, in their native surroundings, they can grow to be the tallest trees in the world. The stream which meanders through the woodland to the right of the track is bordered by alders which in periods of high rainfall, will be partially submerged. This does not harm them, indeed their water resistant trunks have been used in the past as piling or supports for wharves and landing gangways.

Close to Cottenham Farm in the damp grassland amongst stumps of recently felled woodland there are two plants which are often found together in hedgerows and woodland. Red campion with rose-pink petals produces paler pink varieties when it interbreeds with white campion, a separate species also found in the same habitat. These campions are related to the now rare corn field weed, corncockle (Walk 4). Hedge woundwort is easily distinguished by its dark red flowers with a hooded upper lip, a feature shared by the related deadnettles, mints and salvias. Its leaves have a strong

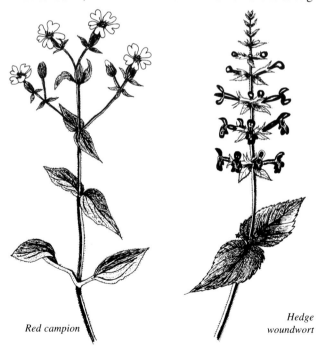

Red campion

Hedge woundwort

81

astringent smell when crushed and were once used for dressing wounds, hence the name.

Cottenham Farm has a more modest 20th century version of the 19th century landscape scheme at Great Tew park, with a new lake, specimen trees and lawn. In the past there was a water mill near here, the water coming through a tunnel from now derelict lakes.

As you walk uphill past Cottenham Farm, on a quiet road created by Loudon in about 1810, notice the gorse below the woodland to the right. This may be a remnant of limestone heath since a map made in 1774 shows this area to be rough pasture.

2. SP404313

At the main road cross with care and take the track opposite leading to Hill Farm. At the farm go left round the barns and through a metal gate to follow the track round the field edge and down hill. Bear right to meet the hedgeline. Turn right and walk with the hedge on the left for 200m. Turn left and cross a stile to walk with a hedge on your left until it curves away from the straight line. Here turn right across the field and head for the gate in the middle of the fence line at the foot of the hill. Through this gate carry on in the same direction to the gate on the skyline up the hill. Carry straight on with the hedge on your left, then into a grassy lane between hedges leading to a gate on to the road. At the road turn left.

The road you cross and re-cross is the former 18th century turnpike between Chipping Norton and Deddington. Turnpike Trusts were set up in the 18th century to improve the poor state of existing main roads. Shareholders put in funds and hoped to make a profit from tolls charged to users. Most old turnpikes are still main roads, although a few have declined in importance.

At Hill Farm look out for a greyish-green plant growing typically on disturbed ground where animal manure has been stored. This is fat hen, whose leaves and seeds were eaten as a food plant for centuries.

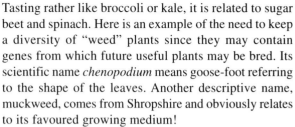

Tasting rather like broccoli or kale, it is related to sugar beet and spinach. Here is an example of the need to keep a diversity of "weed" plants since they may contain genes from which future useful plants may be bred. Its scientific name *chenopodium* means goose-foot referring to the shape of the leaves. Another descriptive name, muckweed, comes from Shropshire and obviously relates to its favoured growing medium!

Just beyond Hill Farm, there is a wide view over the area towards Banbury. The church towers of Barford St John and St Michael are to the right (Walk 7). The steep slopes along this ridge give rise to many springs as the underlying geology changes from marlstone to impervious clay. This can be seen on both sides of the ridge and is noticeable here in changes in the vegetation with rushes growing in the damp areas. Note also how the road crossed earlier, an ancient route, follows the ridge which would be dry underfoot in winter compared with the wetter

Fat hen land on the clay. Iron Down, further east (left) as you climb back uphill, was possibly the site of a Romano-British settlement as finds have been made in this vicinity. The hollows and hummocks below this ridge may indicate the site of former ironstone quarries.

3. SP412314

At the road turn left and walk with care to a track leading off to the right towards Upper Grove Ash Farm. Follow this round the back of the farm buildings then through a gate, following the bridleway along the edge of the field, keeping the hedge on your right. The route continues along the edge of woodland and then down hill straight across a field. Go through more trees and over a stream, carrying straight on down a green lane. At the end of this, turn left following the bridleway along a field edge to the road.

The farm road leads down the other side of the ridge just seen near Hill Farm. However this side of the ridge was once more populated with a village called Grove.

Not mentioned in the Domesday Book, Grove was a
hamlet of Great Barton as was Ledwell close by. In 1279
there were 16 households here but the site slowly
decreased in size between about 1450 and 1700.
Brasenose College bought a house here in 1538 together
with 120 acres of land; the main produce seems to have
been wool. Signs of this earlier habitation may be
apparent in the right light conditions - look for ridge
and furrow, for bumps and hollows in the ground
indicating where houses were situated, or for an oval
hollow marking a lost fish pond. The house present here
today was built in the 17th century as was the one across
the valley at Lower Grove Ash Farm.

The woodland here contains sweet or Spanish chestnut
trees, a species introduced by the Romans. Its serrated,
spear shaped leaves distinguish it from the unrelated
horse chestnut, which has palmate leaves arising from a
stalk like the fingers of a hand. The horse chestnut's
shiny conkers are inedible but sweet chestnut produces
edible nuts in a prickly case, best tried after a frost.
Sweet chestnut is still often grown elsewhere in the
country as coppice to produce stakes for fencing and
hop poles.

In this vicinity, a green woodpecker may be seen
moving between wood and grassland with a character-

Green woodpecker

*Nest of peacock
caterpillars*

istic undulating flight. These birds may be seen feeding on the ground tearing open ant hills, while its long rough tongue extracts the insects and their grubs. Its alarm call resembles human laughter, earning it the country name of yaffle. Unlike its smaller great spotted cousin, it seldom produces the incredibly rapid pecking or drumming sound, although it too may hammer away at trees in search of wood boring insects or when excavating a nest site.

On grassy paths in wet weather, several species of slugs can often be seen which vary in size and colour from large black or orange to small pale brown. Slugs are molluscs and are basically snails minus the shells. As well as eating plant material, they act as waste disposers, devouring faeces from birds and animals, being particularly useful in removing dog droppings from urban areas. In turn slugs are eaten by hedgehogs and birds such as thrushes, which can be at risk from garden pesticides accumulated in them.

Along the field bridleway in midsummer, look out for

dark web-like nests of peacock or small tortoiseshell caterpillars on stinging nettles in the hedgerow. Peacock caterpillars are entirely black, small tortoiseshell are yellow-flecked. These butterflies lay their eggs in clusters which leads to the large groups of caterpillars. Red admiral and comma butterflies also lay their eggs on nettles but singly, rather than in clusters.

4. SP421299

At the road, don't leave the field but take the other path diagonally back across the same field, to eventually cross a footbridge. Continue, heading gradually up hill in the same direction, passing through a hedge and over another footbridge to a gap in a hedge. Continue with the hedge on your right. At the next junction of paths turn right through a gate with a wall on your left back to Great Tew. At the Falkland Arms, turn right for a few metres and then cross the small green to reach the car park.

As the path climbs away from the valley, look across to the right to see views of Grove Ash Farm and the small wood on Raven Hill which you just walked through. The stream at the bottom of the valley is marked by a line of trees which stand out in a mostly arable countryside. This landscape has changed over the years. The green lane which you followed earlier originally continued straight across these fields to join another track which is now the Nether Worton road. This was still the case in the 1830's. Thus the footpath you are now following is relatively new.

Close to the junction of paths in an area of rougher grassland you may see a small black moth flying in May and June. This is the aptly named chimney sweeper moth which is uncommon in this country. Its caterpillar feeds on small umbelliferous plants (carrot family) such as the pignut (see Walk 8).

The wall which is on the left of the path marks the boundary of Great Tew. This is the original pre-Loudon park, created in the 16th century and becoming a deer park in the 18th century. Look over the wall for glimpses of fine specimen trees, able to grow to their full size and shape in the open grassland. Two stone pillars mark a former gateway into the deer park and the map of 1774 depicts an avenue of trees leading from the park northwards past the site of Cottenham Farm to the Chipping Norton to Deddington road. The avenue ran through the field on the right until recent times.

The Falkland Arms is a reminder of the former Lord of the Manor of Great Tew, Lucius Cary, Second Viscount Falkland. He was a royalist comander during the Civil war and died at the Battle of Newbury in 1643.

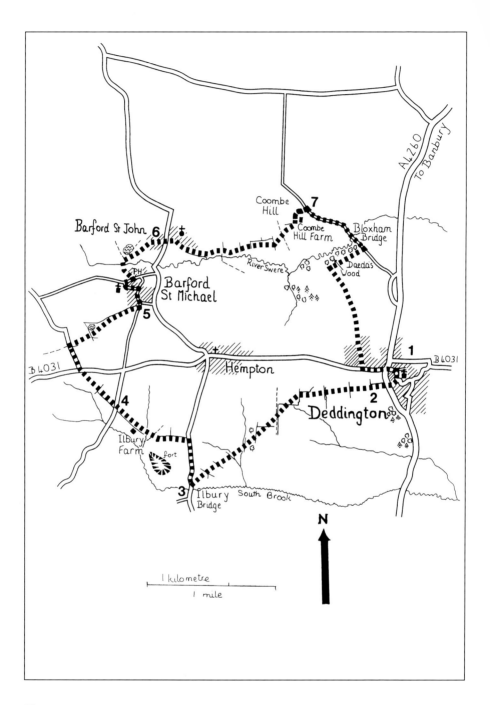

To Banbury

A4260

Coombe Hill **7**

Coombe Hill Farm

Bloxham Bridge

Barford St John **6**

River Swere

Daeda's Wood

PH

Barford St Michael

5

B4031

Hempton

Deddington

1

B4031

4

2

Ilbury Farm

fort

3 Ilbury Bridge

Ilbury South Brook

N

1 kilometre

1 mile

Deddington and the Barfords

8 miles   13 km

This walk passes through an open landscape before descending to the valley to follow the river. It ends with a climb back to Deddington.

1. SP467317

Starting from the Market Place in the centre of Deddington, take Hudson Street in the south west or lower right hand corner. At the main road cross over and take Grove Lane almost opposite.

Deddington, the Saxon village of Daeda's people, was probably settled in the 6th or 7th century. By 1086 it was one of the largest settlements in Oxfordshire and soon after a castle was built. Situated at the crossing of the roads linking Oxford and Banbury, and Buckingham and Chipping Norton, by 1275 Deddington was a borough and a market centre. However, Banbury soon became a more important town and Deddington, although always an important local centre, remained rural rather than urban.

The oldest part of the settlement was to the east of the Market Place around the church and castle site, but larger plots were laid out along New Street, now the

St. Peter and St. Paul,
Deddington

Deddington Town Hall

A4260, in the later Middle Ages when the town became a borough. The buildings here now are mostly 16th or 17th century farmhouses, often incorporating remnants of earlier buildings, which were converted later to other uses.

As well as weekly markets held up to the 19th century, fairs took place here. Originally there were two annual fairs, the most important being held in November. This one continued until the 1930's. In the 19th century it was primarily a cattle fair with droves of Welsh sheep and Irish horses as well as local animals. It was commonly known as the Pudding Pie Fair where this local delicacy was sold, a sort of bread pudding encased in a hard suet crust, hence its name. These were made up to the 1930's despite several uncomplimentary stories and jokes about them! At the end of the route you will return to the starting point via Horse Fair where the horses were sold.

2. SP465316

Continue as Grove Lane becomes a grassy track, then a path which roughly follows the line of electricity poles. Cross a track in a dip, through a gap in the hedge, then continue slightly diagonally left uphill. When you reach a hedge go through a gap ahead. Go diagonally left across the next field, then through a gap in the hedge on the left. Bear right across the next field uphill aiming between the poles on the horizon to reach another track. Cross this and continue in the same direction as before (i.e. slightly left) across the field. When you reach a wooded area, carry on down a short steep path through trees and bushes to emerge in a small valley. Bear left down the bank and left across the field to the opposite hedge, down a steep bank to cross a stile and footbridge. Continue in the same direction across the corner of the next field crossing another stile and footbridge. In the next large field, the path carries on as before to the road. Here turn right.

These large arable fields are virtually devoid of wild

Linnet

flowers and traditional farmland songbirds such as skylarks, yellowhammers, finches and linnets. Further along though, a small wooded valley with a spring echoes to the sound of birdsong. Another patch of uncultivated land supports a host of wild flowers including beaked hawk's beard, germander speedwell, white campion and cranesbill, with its blue flowers. Their seed heads will help sustain farmland birds. However, the much maligned oilseed rape may actually be helping to increase the numbers of linnets in some parts of the country as recent studies have indicated that rape seeds are forming part of their food supply. These oases of uncultivated land are a valuable wild life resource among the surrounding intensively cultivated fields. However such isolated patches need to be linked by uncultivated field margins, headlands or aptly named "beetle banks" to be more effective in sustaining a more diverse wild population of plants, birds, animals and insects.

3. SP442303

At the road turn right (a few metres left will take you to Ilbury Bridge over the South Brook). Follow the road uphill, then turn left along a public Right of Way. Pass through two gates and the yard of Ilbury Farm.

The road is an old one and led originally to a ford over the South Brook, the bridge being built by the 19th century. The bridge still has some Victorian brickwork with dark blue and red bricks, obviously different to more recent replacements.

The fields each side of the road just north of Ilbury Bridge hide the site of Ilbury, a lost hamlet belonging to the parish of Deddington. Named after the Iron Age hillfort or *burh* on the hill to the left, Ilbury was mentioned in the Domesday Book, but declined in size after about 1300. It is not known why the hamlet was depopulated. The land here was later used as sheep pasture with a farm, known as Shepherd's House, situated below the hill fort in the middle of fields, which were inclosed in the 14th century. These fields were a marked contrast to most of the rest of Deddington parish which had open fields until Parliamentary enclosure in 1808. The modern Ilbury Farm was built in the early 20th century on the site of an 18th century barn.

Spear thistle

Notice as you climb uphill how the road is sunk between steep banks on either side, showing how its long use eroded away the ground before it was tarred. This section was situated amongst the old enclosed fields of Ilbury, and contrasts with the wider verges of the road further along where it ran through the open fields; the hedge and verge here were probably not laid out until after 1808.

Look in the verges and footpath edges for two different types of thistle. The spear thistle can grow up to 2m (6 feet) tall and has lance shaped leaves tipped by formidable spines. The large crimson flowerheads are the likely model for Scotland's floral emblem. In contrast, the welted thistle has spiney "wings" along its stems and smaller pale pink flower heads.

The Right of Way is bordered by a tall thick hedgerow containing several native trees and dead stumps of others which provide a versatile habitat for wildlife. The living trees and shrubs provide nest sites and shelter for a variety of birds and small mammals, while berries and

Welted thistle

93

other autumn fruits give sustenance during the winter months. Dead wood is colonized by many kinds of insects, spiders and worms which attract woodpeckers and other insectivorous birds.

As you descend along the track towards the farm, look to the right and beside the farm to see remains of ridge and furrow cultivation in the fields (see Introduction). This is a reminder of the method of ploughing which would have been used in the Middle Ages when Ilbury was a small but thriving community. Just past the farm the ridges change direction, indicating a boundary between two furlongs, or sections of the large, open field. Notice also how the ridges and furrows have a slight reverse S-bend curve. Once the fields were abandoned for arable crops, they were used for pasture and have probably not been ploughed since, certainly not by modern machinery.

4. SP432312

Cross the road and go straight on. At the next road take the lane opposite. Look out for the footpath leading off to the right after about 300 metres. Follow this to Barford St Michael diagonally left across the field.

The hedge alongside the footpath to Barford St Michael marks the old boundary between the open fields and the land belonging to the lord of the manor to the north, the demesne. This land was enclosed with hedges, probably in the late 15th or early 16th century as it was gradually converted to sheep pasture. The many species to be seen in this hedge demonstrate its age - see how many different shrub or tree species you can count in 30 metres. A rough rule of thumb is that one species represents a hundred years in the age of the hedge. You may notice hawthorn with smooth lobed leaves and two stigmas in the flowers, followed by berries with two seeds, different from common hawthorn with serrated leaves and single seeded fruit. This is Midland or woodland hawthorn and is found in old hedges, either formed from woodland or planted with woodland

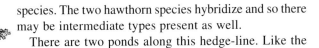

species. The two hawthorn species hybridize and so there may be intermediate types present as well.

There are two ponds along this hedge-line. Like the uncultivated patches seen earlier, such ponds often support more wildlife than the intensively managed farmland. Water-dependent plants and insects such as damsel flies and dragonflies may breed here. Wildfowl, frogs, newts and many birds and small mammals living in the surrounding countryside will benefit from areas of open water such as these. Farm ponds were originally created for watering stock, as flight ponds to attract wildfowl, and for fire fighting. They were often formed when minerals, particularly clay were extracted.

Along the base of the hedge in the ditch, hemlock with its purple blotched stems can be found. This is a highly poisonous member of the carrot family, with attractive ferny leaves, distinguished by a rank mousy smell. This deters livestock from eating it so that in actual fact cases of accidental poisoning are rare.

Hemlock

5. SP434324

When the path meets the road turn left into the village of Barford St Michael. Continue left along Church Street, past St Michael's church then right at the next junction. At the footpath sign turn left following the signs down Mill Lane. This becomes a narrow path at the end beside gardens. Go over the bridge and stile, crossing the infant River Swere, then right along a wire fence, parallel to a large pond. Cross a stile and footbridge, through a gap in the hedge and go diagonally right across a field. Cross another bridge, go right, then left for 100m before turning right, down a track into Barford St John.

The name Barford means "barley ford" and shows the importance of the river crossing here to early settlers. Originally the two Barford hamlets were in different parishes, Barford St John belonging to Adderbury parish, but after several boundary changes they became a single

civil parish in 1932. Both villages stand well above the
river on drier land away from any risk of flooding. The
modern houses in Barford St Michael blend well with
the older ones, with stone or reconstituted stone being
used to match the materials of the old dwellings.

Barford St. John's church

It is worth pausing to look at St Michael's church. It
is built on a large mound and has a Norman doorway
with typical decoration of the period.

The pond and streams form an attractive area in this
quiet valley and provide a good habitat for wildlife, the
still and flowing water fulfilling different needs for a
range of aquatic plants, insects and animals

6. SP438332

In Barford St John, cross the road and take the lane almost opposite, continuing in the same direction as before. The track leads through a farm then along the river. Continue as the track leads away from the river and climbs up to Coombe Hill Farm. Through a gate, follow the path round the back of barns, through another gate, then right across the field to the road.

On the wall of the Manor House to the left, look for a plant with reddish stems. This is pellitory-of-the-wall, its Latin name meaning "wall dweller". In the past it was an important medicinal herb as it was believed to break up kidney or bladder stones because of its association with stone.

Look over the wall on the right as you head out of the village. The bumpy ground indicates the remains of a once larger settlement. There are traces of an earlier manor house with a moat and earth banks of a fortified

Pellitory of the wall

dwelling. The raised areas are platforms where houses were situated and the hollows the tracks between them. The present Manor House was rebuilt in 1920, but the least restored south gable end still bears the date 1598.

The river Swere alongside the track is a tributary of the larger River Cherwell. Two of Britain's largest water birds, the mute swan and the heron, may be seen here. They are unlikely to compete for either nest sites or food as the swans feed mainly on aquatic vegetation, while the herons seek fish, frogs and beetles. Herons nest in tree top colonies, whereas swans build huge nests of reeds or other plant material on river banks or islands. Before the 20th century all swans belonged to the sovereign, monasteries or rich landowners. In this century many swans escaped from captivity and have bred throughout the countryside. However those on the Thames still belong either to the Queen or the Ancient Companies of Dyers or Vinters based in the City of London.

The track along the river is again a pleasant, easy walk. The building you pass is a water mill - notice the built up banks of the mill leat which channelled water to the mill.

As the path rises, across the river valley is the site of a Romano-British settlement, possibly a village. Another similar site is situated to the west of the Barford St Michael.

7. SP455336

At the road turn right and walk downhill. Just after crossing the river at Bloxham Bridge, turn right into Daeda's Wood. Follow the path through the trees, then at the track turn right, and after 400m, left, uphill along a bridleway which bears left to join a track leading back to Deddington. Go straight on between houses. When you reach the main road, turn left to the crossroads and carry straight over to follow the road back to the starting point.

Daeda's Wood is a new community woodland named after the Saxon chieftain who founded Deddington.

Designed and planted in 1996 by local people with the support of local councils, World Wide Fund for Nature and the Forestry Authority, this was the first scheme in the Woodland Trust's "Woods on your Doorstep" project. This was initiated to create new woodlands across England and Wales in celebration of the millennium. The mixture of broad-leaved trees and the wildflower meadow is being managed for wildlife as well as enhancing the local landscape.

*Commemorative plaque,
Deddington*

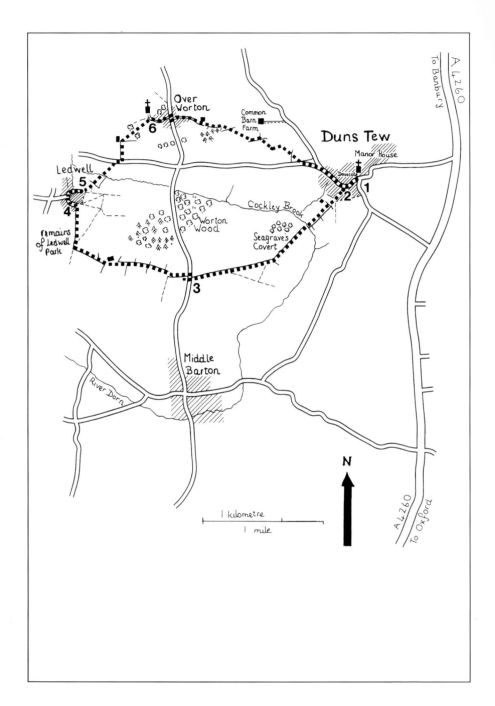

Over Worton

Duns Tew

Manor House

Common Barn Farm

Dovecote

Ledwell

5

4

remains of Ledwell Park

Cockley Brook

Worton Wood

Seagraves Covert

6

3

1

2

Middle Barton

River Dorn

To Banbury

A4260

To Oxford

A4260

N

1 kilometre

1 mile

Duns Tew and Worton

6 miles   10 km

This route passes through two attractive villages, with some good views on the way. Worton Wood is a feature throughout as the route effectively circles it. There are two climbs but the majority of the route is easy walking. Parts of the way can be muddy in wet weather.

1. SP457284

Facing the church in the centre of Duns Tew, go left past Daisy Hill Farm. Continue to the White Horse Inn and take the bridleway to the left alongside.

Duns Tew was listed in the Domesday Book of 1086 in the same entry as Great and Little Tew, all under the heading of Tew. The name "Tew" may refer to a long ridge, such as the one followed by the line of the road west from the village. By the early 14th century there were two sets of field systems (see Introduction), a West end and a Down end. This was reflected in the organisation of the village itself, with different officials for the west and east sides; each end had its own pound. This walk covers the west end of the parish. Daisy Hill Farm which you pass on the left, was one of three village based farms which had their land spreading out behind them.

As you walk through the village, notice the appearance of the buildings. The older houses are built of local ironstone or limestone, while the most modern ones reflect this local character in the colour of the materials used and their design. The medieval dovecote, roofed with Stonesfield slate, stands at the entrance to Duns Tew Manor, although until about 1881 the entrance was further east opposite the small green.

2. SP455283

After 100m pass through a small gate, along a narrow path, then turn right on to a track. Follow this for about 1.5 km (1.0 mile), crossing Cockley Brook and climbing uphill to a gap in the hedge. Go straight on, keeping the hedge on your right, and at a junction of paths continue as before until you reach the road.

This track, earlier known as Witney Way, follows high ground between two damp valleys. From here variations in soil can be seen with red earth from underlying ironstone and farther away to the left, old sand quarries, indicated by gorse growing on the acid soil. A geological fault runs roughly along this line through the village, separating the oolitic limestone and sand to the south from the lias clay and marlstone to the north (see Introduction).

In the past the track ran through the open arable fields, the hedges probably being planted after enclosure in 1794. In the spring these hedges are colourful with apple blossom. Such apples may be the truly wild crab apple, the ancestor of cultivated varieties, or else "wildings" grown from domestic apples. These numerous bushes would imply that they were planted deliberately when the hedges were made at enclosure, as happened in some other parts of the country. Wildings have enormous variation as apples have to cross-pollinate to bear fruit. They often produce fruit which echo old lost varieties or can even produce new varieties. Bramleys, Cox's Orange Pippin and Worcester Pearmain and many more are all varieties from chance seedlings.

As you climb uphill from the brook, the small patch

Grey partridge (left) and red legged partridge

of woodland on the right is Seagrave's Covert, a name implying an area deliberately planted as cover for game birds or foxes to enable hunting. Partridges and pheasants may be seen hereabouts in small numbers. You are more likely to glimpse the red-legged partridge than the native grey species. The former was imported from France in the late 18th century following decimation of the native bird through excessive shooting. Distinguished from the smaller grey by its leg colouration and its chestnut striped flanks, this bird is seen through the summer in family groups of about a dozen flying rapidly before gliding to earth with down-curved wings. Partridges are now in decline probably due to pesticides killing off insect food for chicks, loss of hedgerow cover and absence of winter stubble which formerly provided grain and weed seed for adult birds.

The brook was the boundary between Duns Tew and Westcot Barton; parish boundaries often follow water courses and that to the north and east of the village also follow streams. The hedge you pass through and walk alongside marks the parish boundary between Westcot Barton and Steeple Barton. Such thick old hedges are good habitats for birds. One to listen for is the yellowhammer with its distinctive song "A little bit of bread and no cheese". This sparrow sized bird, with its very obvious yellow head, is, like the partridge, dependent on winter stubble and unmown field edges. It has declined in areas where modern farming practices

Yellowhammer

no longer provide these features. In autumn the hedge is colourful with drapes of shiny red berries of black bryony. This plant is the only British member of the yam family, whereas white bryony belongs to the cucumber family. Both these plants are very poisonous.

Notice along the path here that the soil has changed again and is now stony and brown. You may find fossils in the limestone fragments.

3. SP435271

At the road turn right then left on to another track. Continue along this, eventually passing farm buildings, through a gate at the corner of the wall, then bear right along a grassy track to the right side of a wall ahead. Go through a small gate and continue straight on with the hedgeline on your left to a wall where you turn right. Follow the path along the line of the wall, then through two small gates until you reach a lane.

The mixture of farm buildings are of different time periods. Those built of brick are likely to be Victorian and include one with red brick arches which was a cart hovel, used to shelter farm carts. Above was a granary.

These buildings contrast with the tall open sided Dutch barn and the grey metal modern farm building.

The barn and nearby dry stone walls are encrusted with lichens, some *foliose* or leaflike and some *crustose* or crustlike. They can also be found on the surface of headstones in local churchyards and are more abundant in parts of the countryside where the air is less polluted with sulphur dioxide and other emissions. There is a succession in colonisation by different types; an expert can confirm the age of the stonework from the species present.

Three ferns growing on these walls are easily distinguished by their shapes and colour. Bright green polypody has a clearly divided frond and is named after its much branching root system – literally "many feet". It is often seen growing on the trunks of older trees; this growth form is called epiphytic where one plant grows on another without doing it any harm. In contrast the rustyback fern has olive green fronds, whose lower surfaces are covered in rust coloured scales. The diminutive wall rue spleenwort has very small diamond shaped frond segments. Originating in the north and west of Britain this fern has spread throughout the country, the tiny spores sometimes being carried along the railway network.

From left: Rusty back, Wall rue, Polypody ferns

Look over the wall alongside as you turn right. There are remains of stone columns and walls. These are all that is left of Ledwell Park, which was created in the early 18th century but abandoned less than 100 years later when the mansion was demolished in about 1800, leaving only outbuildings.

The bumpy grassland to the right of the path contains two plants which demonstrate its antiquity. Pignut is a member of the carrot family or umbellifers. It is so called because of its edible tubers, swollen roots storing starchy food which tastes rather like young hazel nuts. Digging up these tubers used to be a favourite pastime of country children but is now illegal. Meadow saxifrage occurs in undisturbed and old grasslands and can be found in some churchyards in this region. Here it can also grow on the limestone walls, so relating to its Latin name of saxifraga – stone breaker, due to the growth of most species of this family in crevices in rocks. This leads to the old fallacy that it can split open stone. Field woodrush is another plant to look for here, most noticeable in spring, when it produces heads of brown flowers in the short grass. Related to true rushes, woodrush has flat hairy leaves instead of the typical round "leaves" of true rushes which are really smooth stems. Its other names of Good Friday grass and cuckoo-grass indicate both its appearance and flowering season.

At the first small gate, notice the fossil shell in the stone on top of the wall alongside.

Meadow saxifrage

4. SP421281

At the lane turn left. Follow the road then turn right at the next junction. Next to the well turn left then right in front of a cottage, and follow a path between walls.

This village is Ledwell, the name meaning "loud stream". There used to be six wells here, this well and pump is the last survivor. Mains water did not come to the village until 1966.

As you leave the village notice the bumpy ground over the wall to the left. This is likely to indicate that

Pignut

Buzzard

the village was once larger than now; this uneven ground hides remains of dwellings. Ledwell was mentioned in the Domesday Book, but was badly hit by Black Death during the 14th century when the population dropped considerably.

In the vicinity of Ledwell you may see one of our largest birds of prey as well as one of the smallest. Both have declined in numbers in many parts of Britain during this century, but have recovered in recent years. Both birds are now protected under wildlife legislation, helped by a generally more enlightened attitude to birds and other wild animals. The buzzard was shot, trapped or

Sparrowhawk

poisoned, being seen as a threat to game birds. However most of their prey is rabbits and other small mammals, the buzzard population being closely linked to that of rabbits. The much smaller sparrowhawk suffered a dramatic decline in the 1960's due to the accumulation of toxic pesticides in its prey. It does not hover like a kestrel but flies low over hedges to surprise the small birds that are its prey. Long term studies show no evidence that they seriously deplete numbers of such birds.

5. SP421282

Cross a stile into the field, walk diagonally left downhill to the hedge at the bottom and pass through a metal gate. Continue diagonally right over the next field to a footbridge over the stream in the right corner. Follow the path diagonally right uphill to the road. Turn right for 50m then left down a farm track. At the end of the track go right through a gate. Over a stile, go diagonally left across the field heading for the gate halfway down the field between two areas of recent tree planting. Through this continue in the same direction to the gate by the large trees onto the road at Worton.

To detour to see the church and other features turn left.

To continue back to Duns Tew turn right.

The first fields after leaving Ledwell contain ridge and furrow (see Introduction). Particularly in the wet hollows, it is easy to see how the ridges helped to keep soil drier than that in the furrows, which are often marked by lines of rushes.

The ridgetop road was known as Churchway in the 15th century or earlier and possibly implies a link between Duns Tew and the church at Great Tew. The road is a vantage point for views of the surrounding countryside with the parkland of Great Tew to the west and Worton Wood to the south. This woodland was once common pasture called the heath but parts were wooded, hence its present day status of "ancient woodland",

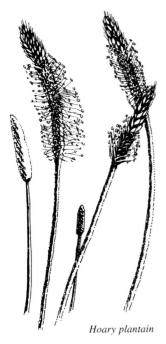

Hoary plantain

accorded to woodland with continuous tree cover for more than 400 years. Planting after 1760 altered the character of the area; in the 19th century it was referred to as "dear to fox-hunters".

Worton contains three large houses, the Rectory, Over Worton House and the Grange, all rebuilt during the early part of the 19th century upon older sites. This was part of a general rebuilding of the village by the Wilson family.

The church of the Holy Trinity was rebuilt in 1844 and is sited close to an Anglo-Saxon burial mound. The church yard contains primroses, bluebells, plantains and ox-eye or moon daisies. This latter species is one of the first meadow flowers to re-establish itself in previously sprayed grassland and is increasingly seen in roadside verges and in set-aside fields. Before leaving the churchyard, look over the hedge to the right. There are traces of terraces of the old garden belonging to Worton House, as well as more ridge and furrow. Views further away include the steep hill of Ilbury fort to the north which will be passed in Walk 7.

6. SP430291

Follow the lane through Over Worton, crossing the minor road and continuing in the same direction. Passing between stone pillars, walk along a drive, lined with Turkey oaks. At Rest Hill House turn right to cross a small area of grassland and pass through a gate in the garden wall. Walk through the garden parallel to the house and exit through a wooden gate (please respect the owner's privacy). Continue straight on to a stile in the corner of the field. Cross the track, go through a gate into a field. Follow the sign and walk straight on along the hedgeline. Cross a stile, then go diagonally right to a gap in the hedge, continuing over the next field in the same direction. At the hedge turn left and follow along it to a gap on the right. Go through into the next field and follow the path diagonally left in the same general direction as before. Go through another gap in the hedge and

continue to a stile onto the road. At the road turn left to return to Duns Tew.

As the path climbs back to Duns Tew look left for views over a typical enclosure landscape. The hillside was common meadow and pasture until 1794, and acted as a division between the two large arable fields of the West end of Duns Tew to the north and south. The path roughly follows the line of the boundary between West End Common and the south field. In the 17th century corn was grown in the north field in even numbered years, synchronising with the north field in Down end, the eastern half of Duns Tew. Common Barn Farm which you can see below was built after enclosure, its name now the only indication of this earlier landscape.

As you walk you may notice flattish stones in the fields here. These were formed from concretions in mud sediments, laid down during the Jurassic period. The action of bacteria in the sediment caused iron carbonate to become iron oxide.

Acknowledgements

This book was written and researched by Mary Webb, Alan Spicer (retired) and Allister Smith, of Oxford Brookes University, and was illustrated by Louise Spicer.

The authors are grateful for help from the staff of the Countryside Service of the Oxfordshire County Council and the Centre for Oxfordshire Studies and to Dr. Alan Childs of Oxford Brookes University for advice on the geology of the area.

The project was sponsored by the Council for the Protection of Rural England, Oxfordshire County Council and Oxford Brookes University.

OXFORD
BROOKES
UNIVERSITY

CPRE

Your countryside – your voice

C P R E Membership

Name _____

Address _____

_____

Postcode

Return completed forms to

**CPRE, FREEPOST,
GOLDTHORPE,
ROTHERHAM S63 9BR**

☐ Yes, I want to help CPRE's work for our countryside. Please enrol me as a member as indicated below *(tick as appropriate)*

SUBSCRIPTIONS

☐ Individual	£17.50	☐ Affiliated organisation	£17.50
☐ Joint	£23.00	☐ Life	£510.00
☐ Under 25	£12.50	☐ Joint life	£730.00
☐ Family membership	£27.50	☐ Over-65 life	£300.00

I would like to make an additional gift of £

Total £

You can increase the value of your gift by 31.58% AT NO EXTRA COST TO YOURSELF. See overleaf.

I would like my subscription to help CPRE's work in *(county of your choice)*

OR

☐ I do not wish to become a member, but wish to help CPRE defend the countryside. Here is my donation of £

☐ I wish to pay by direct debit (see form overleaf)

CPRE (and its agencies) will hold mailing information on its supporters in order to keep them informed of its activities, except in the case of supporters who request otherwise, selected voluntary organisations may be allowed access to such mailing information for one time only, to enable them to send details of their services. CPRE does not in any case sell or rent out this information. Details are held by the DATA Protection Registrar Registered charity number 233179

☐ I enclose a cheque/PO made payable to CPRE

☐ I wish to pay by Access/Visa number

Card expiry date _____ Signature _____

☐ For a free summary of CPRE's policy recommendations on planning, environmental assessment, water, woodlands and forestry, transport, energy, agriculture, mining, landscape protection and other land-use issues, please tick here *(you do not need to join or donate to receive this)*

☐ I do not wish to receive mailings from other selected voluntary organisations

Code: 1025S

DIRECT DEBIT INSTRUCTION

Originator's identification number

7	2	4	2	4	5

DIRECT Debit

Bank _____

Full address of your branch _____

_____ Postcode _____

Name of account holder _____

Your bank account number [ ][ ][ ][ ][ ][ ][ ][ ]

Your bank sort code number [ ][ ][ ][ ][ ][ ]

YOUR INSTRUCTIONS TO THE BANK

Please pay CPRE Direct Debits from the account detailed on this instruction subject to the safeguards assured by the Direct Debit Scheme. (Copies of these safeguards are available from CPRE)

Signature(s) _____ Date _____

Banks and building societies may not accept Direct Debit instructions for some types of account

DEED OF COVENANT (TAX RECOVERY) FORM

To CPRE, I, (Name) _____

of (Address) _____

_____ Postcode _____

promise to pay you each year* such a sum as after deduction of income tax at the basic rate amounts to £ _____ each year, or CPRE's current subscription, whichever is the greater.
(enter the amount you will be giving CPRE annually)

* The Inland Revenue requires that your power to stop making payments should not be exercised for at least four years (unless your death should occur sooner)

Signature _____

Date of signature _____

Ask a friend or relative to witness your signature

Witness' signature _____

Witness' name and address _____

_____ Postcode _____

You can give us the vital, long-term support we need to plan ahead by completing a direct debit. And if you yourself are a taxpayer, covenanting means you can increase the value of your gift by 31.58% at no extra cost to yourself. Just follow these 2 simple steps.

1. Complete the direct debit instruction telling your branch to make payments directly from your account, remembering to sign and date the form.
This allows CPRE to collect your subscription directly from your bank. It saves us money because we don't have to bother you with annual reminders, and your subscription can change without the need for a new mandate each time. We will always tell you in advance if we change your subscription, and you may cancel this authority at any time by advising us and your bank.

2. Complete the covenant (tax recovery) form. You will need to ask someone to witness and sign this form alongside you.

CPRE

Return completed forms to CPRE, FREEPOST, GOLDTHORPE, ROTHERHAM S63 9BR